SHEET CAKE

# SHEET CAKE

## EASY ONE-PAN RECIPES
*for every day & every occasion*

ABIGAIL JOHNSON DODGE

CLARKSON POTTER/PUBLISHERS
NEW YORK

*For Ed Mileti.*
*Your taste buds were missed*
*on this one, buddy.*

CLARKSON POTTER is a trademark
and POTTER with colophon is a
registered trademark of Penguin
Random House LLC.

Library of Congress Cataloging-in-
Publication Data is available upon
request.

ISBN 978-0-593-13610-2
Ebook ISBN 978-0-593-13611-9

Printed in China

Photographer: Lauren Volo
Editor: Michele Eniclerico
Designers: Stephanie Huntwork
and Jan Derevjanik
Production Editor: Patricia Shaw
Production Manager: Jessica Heim
Composition: Merri Ann Morrell
Copy Editor: Carole Berglie
Indexer: Elizabeth T. Parson

Cover design by Stephanie Huntwork
Cover photographs by Lauren Volo

10 9 8 7 6 5 4 3 2 1

First Edition

# contents

# introduction

· · · · · · · · · · · · · · · · · · · · · · · · · · · · · · · · · · · · · · · · · · · · · · · ·

**AS A COOKBOOK AUTHOR, RECIPE DEVELOPER, AND INSTRUCTOR, I'VE**
spent my career streamlining, demystifying, and modernizing
baking for home bakers of all experience levels. My goal is
always to guide you through each recipe, offering all the
instructions, tips, and techniques you'll need for baking with
confidence and success.

*Sheet Cake* exemplifies and highlights this philosophy. Within its
pages you'll discover that one half-sheet pan—the same one you
already own and use for shortcut dinners—is the only pan you need
to create fun and festive cakes that are surprisingly easy to make. No
matter which cake style you choose—classic, stacked, or rolled—it
will bake in a fraction of the time that traditional cake layers take, it
will cool even faster, and it can be ready to serve, in many cases, in
under an hour. I've laid out fifty cakes, teamed with soaks (sometimes
optional), frostings, and, when applicable, fillings, along with some
tasty accompaniments that add to the cake's already great flavors.
With so many fillings and frostings, soaks and sauces, the mix-and-
match options are practically endless. Experiment and have some fun
creating new cake combos.

The goal of these cake recipes is not to create something perfect.
It doesn't matter a lick if your finished cake looks like mine, or if the
roll is cracked or the stacked cake is lopsided, or if the frosting is
speckled with cake crumbs. What you baked with care will still taste
delicious and will tickle the taste buds of your family and friends.

I am always here to help, so if you have questions or need some
baking encouragement, please visit me at www.abbydodge.com and
"Ask Abby." I can't wait to hear from you!

*before we begin*

Whether you are a cake-baking newbie or a seasoned pro, I encourage you to read this section before you turn on your oven. Here you'll find the grocery staples, essential equipment, and indispensable techniques that will help you make your cakes true successes.

## EQUIPMENT: SHEET CAKE TOOLS

### half-sheet pan

All the cakes in this book are baked in a 13 by 18 by 1-inch (33 by 46 by 2.5 centimeter) half-sheet pan made of uncoated aluminum.

### parchment

Lining your sheet pan with silicone-coated parchment, with help from greasing and flouring (see page 17), will eliminate the problem of cakes sticking to the pan, as well as speed up your cleanup. Wax paper is not a substitute!

### kitchen scale

For the most accurate measuring of dry and wet ingredients, as well as proper portioning of batters, I urge you to have and use a scale. Look for one with a flat surface so you can set a bowl on it for weighing ingredients, a button to reset the scale to zero (tare) and that measures in ⅛-ounce (4 g) increments up to 5 pounds (2.3 kilograms). It should also have a readout for ounces as well as grams.

### volume measuring

If you aren't weighing ingredients, you'll need a set of metal measuring cups (sizes from ¼ to 1 cup) for dry ingredients and thicker liquid items (peanut butter, sour cream, Nutella, mascarpone, etc.), and a set of glass and/or plastic measures for thin liquids, such as water, milk, and oil.

You'll also need a set of standard graduated measuring spoons (sizes from ⅛ teaspoon to 1 tablespoon) for liquids and dry ingredients like spices and baking powder.

### mixing bowls

Bowls have a multitude of uses. In addition to mixing and measuring duty, glass heatproof bowls pull extra duty as they can go into the microwave, sit on top of simmering water, and be washed in the dishwasher. I like to have a few metal bowls, too.

## wire whisk

Thin-wired whisks are excellent multitaskers. Small whisks are great for blending dry ingredients, as well as combining wet ingredients in small vessels. Medium whisks are perfect for whisking fillings and larger amounts of liquids.

## stand mixer or handheld

The recipes in this book can be successfully made with a stand mixer, but if you have an electric handheld mixer, feel free to use it. Mixing might take a minute or so longer with a handheld, so remember to follow the sensory cues for doneness.

## spatula

Silicone spatulas are versatile because they are heatproof, unless otherwise labeled, up to 500°F/260°C; but good old rubber works, too.

## offset spatula

Whether you are spreading batter or filling or are frosting a cake, using an offset spatula will make the process easier, faster, and cleaner. You may want to get a small one in addition to a long one for transferring cakes, especially rolled ones, to serving plates.

## pastry brush

I like the multiple layer of bristles in a silicone brush. It spreads a cake soak smoothly and easily, and it's also dishwasher-safe.

## oven thermometer

Just because you have your oven set to a certain temperature does not necessarily mean it is accurate. This discrepancy can have a major impact on your timing and, worse, on your results. Since temperatures are so important in baking, it's not enough to trust the digital readout on your oven. To test your oven, set a thermometer in the center of the oven, preheat it, and check back in 15 to 20 minutes to be sure the temperatures are in sync. Adjust the controls of your oven as needed until the temperature on the thermometer is as desired. You can also have your oven tested by a service repair professional and recalibrated, if necessary.

Keep an eye out for hot spots in your oven. These are pockets that are hotter than other areas and can cause overcooking and even burning. If you can identify these hot spots, you can rotate your pans halfway through the baking time to avoid unevenness.

## microplane zester

Although they come in a variety of shapes and sizes, I like a wide, stainless-steel blade with a rubber-coated grip and small and extremely sharp holes for finely grating citrus zest.

## large wire cooling racks

I recommend having at the ready two racks, both half-sheet size (at least 13 by 18 inches [33 by 46 centimeters], but larger is ideal).

## cake plates

For stacked cakes, you'll need 8- to 10-inch (20 to 25 centimeter) flat rounds, and for the rolled cakes, you'll need rectangular servers in lengths of 14 to 20 inches and at least 6 inches wide (35.5 to 50 centimeters, and at least 15 centimeters in width), depending on how you choose to roll the cakes. Plastic, china, glass, and wooden rounds are all good options. Don't forget about cheese boards in any shape (yup, a round cake on a square, flat cheese board!); they are gorgeous for serving these cakes.

## cake boards

Corrugated cake boards are among my favorite baking assistants. I keep a few 8- and 10-inch (20 and 25 centimeter) rounds and rectangles with a length of 14 to 20 inches and a width of at least 6 inches (35.5 to 50 centimeters, and a width of at least 15 centimeters) in the pantry. For stacked cakes, I trim an 8-inch round to a 6¾-inch (16.5 centimeter) round to serve as a template for cutting out the layers, as well as using as a base for assembling, frosting, and decorating.

## knives

Yup, even bakers need a few good knives. Here are several that I recommend having on hand for making and serving these cakes.

**Medium chef's knife** for chopping and prepping fruit

**9-inch (23 centimeter) utility knife** to slice cakes

**Medium serrated knife** for slicing cakes (see page 21)

**Small paring knife** for prepping fruit or marking and cutting cakes into strips and rounds

## sieves

A medium sieve is used to sift some dry ingredients and to dust cake layers with confectioners' sugar. A fine-mesh mini sieve is great for sifting when desserts are garnished with confectioners' sugar or cocoa.

## ruler

When it comes to baking, a ruler is your best friend. Using a ruler to measure your lengths, widths, and slices is the only way to ensure that your pan, cake strips, or slices are the right size. For these cakes, I use a 20-inch (50 centimeter) ruler frequently.

# KEY INGREDIENTS

## flours

**ALL-PURPOSE FLOUR** · The majority of these cakes calls for unbleached all-purpose flour. I use Gold Medal, Pillsbury, and King Arthur interchangeably for these recipes, all with good results. Because of the chemicals used to whiten flour, I prefer unbleached flour.

**CAKE FLOUR** · For more delicate cakes, a softer wheat flour with a lower protein content can be a better fit. I use Swans Down and I always sift it (sometimes more than once) after measuring.

## sugars

**GRANULATED SUGAR** · Also known as white sugar, it is sometimes made from refined beet sugar, but more commonly it is from refined cane sugar.

**BROWN SUGARS** · Adding varying amounts of molasses to granulated sugar makes both light and dark brown sugar. The darker the sugar, the more molasses it contains. In most recipes, the two types are interchangeable, with the exception that dark brown sugar will give a slightly spicier flavor and a deeper color.

**CONFECTIONERS' SUGAR** · Also known as powdered, 10X, or icing sugar, confectioners' sugar is granulated sugar that has been crushed into a very fine powder and combined with cornstarch to prevent it from clumping. (Lumps will inevitably form, so it should be sifted before using.)

## salts

**TABLE SALT** · I use table salt in all my recipes. Unlike the random sizes of granules in kosher salt, table salt granules are fine and relatively uniform, so measuring is more consistent.

**COARSE SEA SALT** · A sprinkle of coarse sea salt as a finishing touch adds sparkle and kick to a cake. Sea salt is very coarse, in some cases even flaky. Two of my favorites are Fleur de Sel and Maldon.

## butter

These recipes rely exclusively on unsalted butter. It is fresher than its salted counterpart and allows you to accurately control the salt levels when baking.

## eggs

These recipes all call for large eggs. Unless otherwise directed, eggs should be used at room temperature. If you are in a rush and your eggs are cold, you can warm them in a bowl of warm water for a few minutes.

## chocolates

**BAR CHOCOLATE** · I like to bake with bittersweet chocolate that contains 60% to 62% chocolate solids. Most brands, but not all, call this "bittersweet," but do check labels. The higher-percentage choices have more cacao and less

added sugar, giving a stronger, more bitter flavor to the chocolate. Within the 60% to 70% range, bittersweet and semisweet are interchangeable. Scharffen Berger's semisweet and Ghirardelli bittersweet are my favorites.

**CHOCOLATE CHIPS**  I like Guittard and Ghirardelli milk, white, bittersweet, or semisweet chips. I prefer not to substitute chips for chopped bittersweet or semisweet chocolate, but in most cases it can be done successfully. The exception is white chocolate chips; owing to the added stabilizers in white chocolate, the chips will not melt properly.

**COCOA POWDER**  Made from roasted cocoa beans pulverized into a paste and then dried and ground, this fine powder is unsweetened. I prefer natural (not Dutch-process) cocoa; Hershey's is the most commonly available.

### extracts

In all instances, use only pure extracts. Pure vanilla extract and vanilla bean paste can be used interchangeably and in the same amounts.

### dairy

For milk, cream, and sour cream, use whole or full-fat—avoid low-fat products. Buttermilk, however, can be low-fat or fat-free. In a pinch, you can make your own buttermilk by replacing 2 tablespoons of 1 cup whole milk (8 oz/227 g) with 2 tablespoons fresh lemon juice. Give it a stir and let sit for a few minutes before using.

### nuts

I use toasted, unsalted nuts in my batters and dough so as to control the salt levels in the recipes. For garnishing my cakes, I use lightly salted nuts to kick up the sweet flavors in the dessert and push the sweet/savory line. In either case, make sure to toast the nuts, as the process brings out their bolder flavor.

To keep nuts tasting fresh, store them in a heavy-duty zip-top plastic bag in the freezer. They thaw quickly. Unless otherwise indicated, nuts are easily swappable.

### oils

For the majority of recipes that call for an oil, I use the term "neutral" because any one of many unflavored oils—safflower, canola, pure vegetable, corn, and grape-seed—will work well. For recipes that call for olive oil, use a light, fruity oil.

### jams and fruit purees

Tuck a jar or two of your favorite flavors of good-quality jam in your pantry. The same goes for store-bought unsweetened fruit purees. Look for them in the health food, refrigerated, or frozen foods section. They are convenient and will deliver big flavor boosts to your cakes.

### peanut butter

For all the peanut butter recipes in this book, I use processed peanut butter.

# TECHNIQUES FOR EXCELLENT SHEET CAKES

## preparing the pan

**FOR STACKED AND ROLLED CAKES** Lightly grease the bottom and sides of the half-sheet pan. I recommend using a corner of a folded paper towel to spread the oil evenly over the surface so it doesn't pool. Line the bottom with parchment and lightly grease. Lightly flour the bottom and sides of the pan. Turn the pan upside down and tap out any excess flour. Leave the pan upside down until you're ready to fill it to prevent any accidental spills from marring the floured surface while you are preparing the cake.

**FOR CLASSIC CAKES** Follow the same directions, except you can eliminate the parchment liner.

## mise en place

*Mise en place*—French for "put in place"—is the process of organizing and prepping your ingredients so that you are 100 percent sure you have all the ingredients and they are all properly measured so you can work through the recipe smoothly and efficiently.

## how to measure ingredients

**SCALE MEASURING** For the best, most consistent baked results, use the ounce or gram measurements for the dry and liquid ingredients as listed in the recipe. Simply put your bowl on the scale, press the tare button so the scale registers zero, then spoon or pour in your ingredients until the scale reads the appropriate weight. To add other ingredients, keep the bowl on the scale and return your scale to zero again by pressing the tare button for each addition.

**VOLUME MEASURING** If you don't use a scale, use the spoon-and-sweep method for flour (all-purpose and cake), cornstarch, and confectioners' sugar. Stir the ingredient in its container, lightly spoon it into the correct measuring cup (no scooping, packing, or tapping) and sweep off the excess with a flat edge (like the flat side of a knife or a ruler or spatula handle). There are two exceptions to this: for granulated sugar, you can dip and sweep (it will weigh the same), and for brown sugar, you should firmly pack into the appropriate size metal measuring cup.

Liquid measures by volume are best done in a glass or plastic measuring cup with markings you can read when the cup is set on the counter and you are looking straight at it.

## mixing

Whether you are using a stand mixer or handheld, it's prudent to start mixing on a low speed and build up to the speed noted in the instructions. This way, you will avoid having the ingredients spray out of the bowl.

In order to combine the ingredients thoroughly, it's important to occasionally stop mixing and, using a rubber spatula, scrape the batter from the beater and the sides of the bowl.

### checking for doneness

I always give doneness tests (sensory cues) along with a suggested time frame to help you gauge when it's time to move onto the next step and when a recipe is done mixing, baking, or chilling. The time frame should be used as a general guide—it is not a hard-and-fast rule. It's up to you, the person who is smelling, tasting, touching, and looking at what you are making, to make the determination. Using the doneness cue, engage and trust your senses to determine when the recipe is ready. Mark down any changes in the margin so you have it for the next time.

### adding a soak

A soak is a syrup made with sugar, water (or another liquid), and sometimes an additional flavoring. It's used to moisten a cake layer and, if it's flavored, to deliver an extra depth of flavor to the cake. Although using a soak is sometimes optional, it's a great addition if time permits.

### how to make cake croutons

Using a serrated knife, cut the edges of the cake scraps into ¾-inch pieces. For soft croutons, cover and store the pieces at room temperature for up to three days or freeze for up to three months. Thaw at room temperature and refresh in a 350°F (180°C/gas mark 4) oven for about 5 minutes. For crisp croutons, arrange the cake pieces on a parchment-lined half-sheet pan so they aren't touching and bake in a 350°F (180°C/gas mark 4) oven until the edges are dry, 12 to 14 minutes. Set aside to cool completely. The cake croutons can also be mixed into brownie or cookie dough, used in a bread pudding, layered with mousse or whipped cream in a parfait, or sprinkled on top of ice cream.

### how to make cake crumbs

Trim away the edges of the remaining cake pieces from a stacked cake layer and use the edge of a small knife to carefully scrape away any sticky parts, if necessary, from the cake scraps and discard. Using your fingers, gently crumble the cake pieces onto a half-sheet pan or large bowl. The crumbled cake can be in fine or large pieces, depending on your preference. Cover and store at room temperature for up to three days or transfer to a heavy-duty zip-top plastic bag and freeze for up to three months before using. Thaw at room temperature and refresh in a 350°F (180°C/gas mark 4) oven for about 5 minutes. Cake crumbs can also be used for an ice cream topping or mixed with some frosting and rolled in sprinkles to make cake bites.

**STORING**  Almost all the sheet cakes can be served immediately (although they might be soft). If you aren't serving the cake right away, refrigerate it for one hour, cover loosely with plastic, and continue to chill for up to one day before bringing it to room temperature (see next section for timing) and serving unless otherwise noted in the recipe. Leftovers, if there are any, are delicious for days.

**TIMING**  Most cakes need some time out of the fridge before being served to allow some of the chill to dissipate so the flavors and textures can shine. The timing depends on what type of filling and frosting was used. The following is a general guide, but keep in mind that your timing might vary depending on your refrigerator and your ambient kitchen temperature, so adjust accordingly.

**Buttercream** – 2 hours

**Whipped cream** – 30 minutes

**American buttercream** – 1 hour

**Ganache** – 1 hour

**Combination of whipped cream and buttercream** – 1 hour

**Pastry cream** – 30 minutes

**Cream cheese** – 1 hour

## cutting the cake

Clean slices make an elegant presentation. To cut any sticky cake into clean slices, heat the knife, either by dipping it in a tall container of hot water or by holding it under hot running water for a few seconds. Then wipe it dry before cutting. The knife will cool quickly, so expect to wipe the knife clean and rewarm it between cuts. Alternatively, you can do what the pros do and heat your knife over an open flame. Make sure to dedicate one knife as your slicing blade, as the heat will dull its sharpness.

## covering the cake

Cakes are best preserved if covered with a cake cover, an upside-down large bowl, plastic wrap, or for classic cakes, you can use an inverted second half-sheet pan. If using plastic wrap, you can prevent a sticky situation from marring your masterpiece: arrange one or two long pieces (depending on the shape of your cake) of plastic wrap on the counter; lightly grease the general area that will be in contact with the cake; and using the corner of a folded paper towel, spread the oil in a thin layer before loosely but completely covering the cake.

# classic cakes

*Well known for their appearances at parties, potlucks, and* bake sales, classic-style sheet cakes are meant to be cooled in their pan, frosted with a variety of soaks and frostings, garnished (if you choose to do so), and served straight from the pan. They couldn't be easier to make and serve!

All styles of cakes can be made as a classic cake, including some that might surprise you. Here, you'll find traditional butter cakes, sponges, and chiffons; but you'll also find upside-downers and mousse cakes, along with a fruit-studded pound cake and a crumb cake.

The assembly of each classic cake follows a similar path. The following steps are referenced in each recipe; that said, there are a few exceptions given in some instructions, so be sure to read carefully.

## assembling the cake

Remove the cake from the oven and place it on a rack to cool completely. No need to unmold.

If the recipe calls for a soak, use a small pastry brush to brush the liquid evenly over the cake layer. Pile the frosting onto the cake layer and spread evenly to the cake's edge.

Unless otherwise directed, the majority of these cakes can be stored, covered, at room temperature.

## serving the cake

Just before serving, garnish as suggested or have some fun and choose your own toppings, then cut and serve pieces of the cake using a wide offset spatula.

A YELLOW BUTTER CAKE IS ESSENTIAL to every baker's repertoire. The gorgeous yellow color is a standout, but the real star of this show is how wonderfully versatile this cake is, as it pairs perfectly with a multitude of frostings. I paired this one with Vanilla Mascarpone Cream Frosting and fresh berries, but it is just as yummy with the Peanut Butter variation (page 139) of the Classic Cream Cheese Frosting.

## cake

4 cups (18 oz/511 g) **unbleached all-purpose flour**

2½ teaspoons **baking powder**

2 teaspoons **table salt**

¼ teaspoon **baking soda**

2½ sticks (1 cup plus 4 tablespoons/10 oz/ 283 g) **unsalted butter**, softened

2 tablespoons **neutral oil**

2 cups (14 oz/397 g) **granulated sugar**

2 large **eggs**, at room temperature

4 large **egg yolks**, at room temperature

4 teaspoons **pure vanilla extract**

1⅔ cups (13⅜ oz/379 g) **buttermilk**, at room temperature

## assembly and serving

**Vanilla Mascarpone Cream Frosting** (full recipe, with Crushed Fruit add-in using fresh raspberries; pages 145 and 153)

Handful of fresh **berries**, rinsed, dried, and chopped if large

### BAKE THE CAKE

**1.** Position a rack in the center of the oven and preheat the oven to 350°F (180°C/gas mark 4). Lightly grease and flour the bottom and sides of the half-sheet pan.

**2.** Combine the flour, baking powder, salt, and baking soda in a medium bowl and whisk until blended. In the bowl of a stand mixer fitted with the paddle attachment, beat the butter and oil on medium speed until smooth, about 1 minute. Add the sugar and continue beating on medium-high speed until fluffy and lighter in color, 2 to 3 more minutes.

**3.** Add the eggs and 3 of the yolks, one at a time, beating until blended after each addition. Add the vanilla along with the remaining yolk. Add one-third of the flour mixture and mix on low speed until just blended, about 30 seconds. Add half the buttermilk and mix until just blended, about 30 seconds more. Add another third of the flour mixture and mix on low speed until just blended, about 30 seconds. Add the remaining buttermilk and mix until just blended, about 30 seconds. Add the remaining flour mixture and mix until just blended, about 30 seconds.

**4.** Scrape the batter into the prepared pan and, using an offset spatula, spread evenly. Bake until a toothpick inserted in the center comes out clean, 20 to 22 minutes.

**5.** Let the cake cool in the pan.

### ASSEMBLE AND SERVE THE CAKE

**6.** Spread the frosting evenly over the cake layer. Follow the directions for storing and serving the cake (see page 21). Just before serving, scatter the berries on top of the cake.

*serves*
**12 to 16**

**THIS IS A CLASSIC VERSION OF AN AMERICAN FAVORITE.** The carrot-studded cake is moist yet delicate and the spicy, sweet flavors are well balanced. As for the frosting, while I love a good cream cheese frosting when linked with carrot cake, I chose to pair the cake here with an orange buttercream for its delicate flavor and silky texture. If you are craving a more classic coupling, feel free to use the Honey variation (page 139) of the Vanilla Cream Cheese Frosting.

serves
**12 to 16**

## cake

3¼ cups (14⅝ oz/415 g) **unbleached all-purpose flour**

1¼ cups (8¾ oz/248 g) **granulated sugar**

1¼ cups (8¾ oz/248 g) packed **light brown sugar**

2½ teaspoons **ground cinnamon**

¾ teaspoon **baking soda**

1 teaspoon **ground ginger**

1 teaspoon **table salt**

¾ teaspoon **ground nutmeg**

3 cups (11 oz/312 g) coarsely grated **carrots**

1¼ cups (9⅝ oz/273 g) **neutral oil**

6 large **eggs**, at room temperature

1 tablespoon finely grated **orange zest**

2½ teaspoons **pure vanilla extract**

## assembly and serving

**Vanilla Buttercream Frosting** (full recipe, with Citrus add-in using orange zest; pages 150 and 153)

½ cup (2 oz/57 g) finely chopped **walnuts**, toasted (optional)

### BAKE THE CAKE

**1.** Position a rack in the center of the oven and preheat the oven to 350°F (180°C/gas mark 4).

**2.** Lightly grease and flour the bottom and sides of the half-sheet pan.

**3.** Combine the flour, granulated and brown sugars, cinnamon, baking soda, ginger, salt, and nutmeg in the bowl of a stand mixer fitted with the paddle attachment and beat on medium-low speed until well blended, about 1 minute. Add the carrots, oil, eggs, orange zest, and vanilla. Beat on medium-low speed until combined, about 30 seconds. Increase the speed to medium and beat until well blended, about 1 minute more.

**4.** Scrape the batter into the prepared pan and, using an offset spatula, spread evenly. Bake until a toothpick inserted in the center comes out clean, 22 to 24 minutes.

**5.** Let the cake cool in the pan.

### ASSEMBLE AND SERVE THE CAKE

**6.** Spread the frosting evenly over the cake layer. Follow the directions for storing and serving the cake (see page 21). Just before serving, scatter the nuts on top of the cake, if desired.

### flavor swap

**HONEY CREAM CHEESE**  Use the Vanilla Cream Cheese Frosting (full recipe, Honey variation; page 139) in place of the orange-flavored buttercream.

**I LOVE THE ADDITION OF CRUSHED TOASTED COCONUT** to this cake. The scattered flecks of golden brown look like confetti (which is fun) and they add another layer of coconut flavor to an already very coconut-y dessert. If you don't have a can of coconut milk in the pantry, substitute an equal amount of milk and increase the coconut extract to 1 teaspoon. The Whipped Caramel Cream (full recipe, page 147) also makes a yummy topper.

### cake

2½ cups (11¼ oz/319 g) **unbleached all-purpose flour**

¾ cup (1⅞ oz/53 g) **sweetened flaked coconut**, toasted and crushed

1¾ teaspoons **baking powder**

¼ teaspoon **baking soda**

¾ teaspoon **table salt**

2 sticks (1 cup/8 oz/227 g) **unsalted butter**, softened

1¾ cups (12¼ oz/350 g) **granulated sugar**

3 large **eggs**, at room temperature

1 large **egg yolk**, at room temperature

2 teaspoons **pure vanilla extract**

½ teaspoon **coconut extract**

½ cup (4 oz/113 g) **whole milk**, at room temperature

¾ cup (6⅜ oz/181 g) **coconut milk**

### assembly and serving

**White Chocolate Frosting** (full recipe, Coconut variation; page 149)

2 cups (5 oz/142 g) **sweetened flaked coconut**, toasted (optional)

**BAKE THE CAKE**

**1.** Position a rack in the center of the oven and preheat the oven to 350°F (180°C/gas mark 4).

**2.** Lightly grease and flour the bottom and sides of a half-sheet pan.

**3.** Combine the flour, coconut, baking powder, baking soda, and salt in a medium bowl and whisk until blended. In the bowl of a stand mixer fitted with the paddle attachment, beat the butter on medium speed until smooth, about 1 minute. Add the sugar and continue beating on medium-high speed until fluffy and lighter in color, 2 to 3 minutes.

**4.** Add 2 of the eggs and the yolk, one at a time, beating until blended after each addition. Add the vanilla and coconut extract along with the remaining egg. Add one-third of the flour mixture and mix on low speed until just blended, about 30 seconds. Add the milk and mix until just blended, about 30 seconds more. Add another third of the flour mixture and mix on low speed until just blended, about 30 seconds. Add the coconut milk and mix until just blended, about 30 seconds. Add the remaining flour mixture and mix until just blended, about 30 seconds.

**5.** Scrape the batter into the prepared pan and, using an offset spatula, spread evenly. Bake until the top springs back when lightly touched, 20 to 22 minutes.

**6.** Let the cake cool in the pan.

**ASSEMBLE AND SERVE THE CAKE**

**7.** Spread the frosting evenly over the cake layer. Follow the directions for storing and serving the cake (see page 21). Just before serving, scatter the toasted coconut on top of the cake, if desired.

*serves*
**12 to 16**

**THIS CAKE IS ONE OF MY FAVORITES.** It's super simple to make *and* can be prepared in stages days ahead of time. The eggless cake batter mixes in one bowl and bakes into an intensely chocolate-y layer. The mousse is actually a whipped ganache made with only three ingredients and prepared in three easy steps: combine the ingredients, chill, then whip. All that's left is to assemble and let the mousse cake set.

### cake

2 cups (9 oz/255 g) **unbleached all-purpose flour**

1⅓ cups (9⅜ oz /266 g) **granulated sugar**

⅔ cup (2 oz /57 g) **unsweetened natural cocoa powder**, sifted

1½ teaspoons **baking soda**

1 teaspoon **table salt**

1½ cups (12 oz/340 g) **water**

⅓ cup (2½ oz/71 g) **neutral oil**

1 tablespoon **pure vanilla extract**

1 tablespoon **white vinegar**

### assembly and serving

**Classic Soak** (Cream or Chocolate variation; page 156), or ½ cup (5½ oz/ 156 g) raspberry jam

**Bittersweet Chocolate Ganache** (full recipe; page 140)

Handful of fresh **raspberries**

**Chocolate Curls** (page 163)

**Confectioners' sugar** (optional)

### BAKE THE CAKE

**1.** Position a rack in the center of the oven and preheat the oven to 350°F (180°C/gas mark 4).

**2.** Lightly grease and flour the bottom and sides of the half-sheet pan.

**3.** Combine the flour, sugar, cocoa, baking soda, and salt in a large bowl and whisk until blended. Add the water, oil, vanilla, and vinegar and whisk until well blended and smooth, about 2 minutes.

**4.** Scrape the batter into the prepared pan and, using an offset spatula, spread evenly. Bake until a toothpick inserted in the center comes out clean, 12 to 14 minutes.

**5.** Let the cake cool in the pan.

### ASSEMBLE AND SERVE THE CAKE

**6.** Make room in the refrigerator for the half-sheet pan.

**7.** Spread the soak or jam evenly over the cake layer. Spread the ganache onto the cake layer. Refrigerate for 1 hour, then cover loosely and continue to chill until the mousse is firm, at least 3 hours more or up to 2 days before serving.

**8.** Just before serving, scatter the raspberries and chocolate curls on top of the cake and dust with confectioners' sugar, if desired.

### flavor swap

**MOCHA**   Use strong coffee, at room temperature, in place of the water in the cake. Use the Classic Soak (Coffee variation, page 156) along with the Bittersweet Chocolate Ganache (full recipe, Milk Chocolate variation, page 140).

*serves*
**12** *to* **16**

**POUND CAKE IS A YEAR-ROUND DESSERT.** Much like a little black dress that can take you anywhere and to any function, a great pound cake can be a casual picnic snack or the delicious finale to an elegant meal. The cake is moist and stand-alone delicious, but I like folding some lightly crushed fresh fruit into the batter for a vibrant flavor boost.

## topping

½ cup (3½ oz/99 g) **granulated sugar**

½ teaspoon **water**

## cake

2⅔ cups (12 oz/340 g) **unbleached all-purpose flour**

1½ teaspoons **table salt**

1 teaspoon **baking powder**

3 sticks (1½ cups/12 oz/ 340 g) **unsalted butter**, softened

8 ounces (227 g) **cream cheese**, softened

2 cups (14 oz/397 g) **granulated sugar**

⅔ cup (4⅝ oz/131 g) packed **light brown sugar**

6 large **eggs**, at room temperature

4 teaspoons finely grated **orange zest**

1 tablespoon **pure vanilla extract**

2 cups (10 oz/280 g) diced, unpeeled **peaches**

## flavor swap

**BLUEBERRY-LEMON**
Add 1 tablespoon finely grated lemon zest along with the last egg and use 2 cups (10 oz/280 g) fresh blueberries, rinsed, dried, and lightly crushed.

### MAKE THE TOPPING

**1.** Combine the sugar and water in a small bowl and stir until the sugar is evenly moistened and forms small clumps.

### BAKE THE CAKE

**2.** Position a rack in the center of the oven and preheat the oven to 350°F (180°C/gas mark 4).

**3.** Lightly grease and flour the bottom and sides of the half-sheet pan.

**4.** Combine the flour, salt, and baking powder in a medium bowl and whisk until blended. In the bowl of a stand mixer fitted with the paddle attachment, add the butter and cream cheese and beat on medium speed until smooth, about 1 minute. Add the granulated and brown sugars and continue beating on medium-high speed until fluffy and lighter in color, 2 to 3 minutes.

**5.** Add 5 of the eggs, one at a time, beating until blended after each addition. Add the orange zest and vanilla along with the remaining egg. Add half the flour mixture and mix on low speed until just blended, about 30 seconds. Add the remaining flour mixture and mix until just blended, about 30 seconds. Add the peaches and, using a rubber spatula, fold until just blended.

**6.** Scrape the batter into the prepared pan and, using an offset spatula, spread evenly. Sprinkle the topping evenly over the batter. Bake until a toothpick inserted in the center comes out clean, 33 to 35 minutes.

**7.** Let the cake cool in the pan.

**8.** Slice and serve or cover and store at room temperature for up to 4 days.

*serves*
**12 to 16**

**HAVE YOU HEARD OF A DUSTY SUNDAE**, aka Dusty Miller Sundae? It's my favorite childhood ice cream treat that endures to this day. Pile a scoop or three of vanilla ice cream into a dish, top with a solid amount of chocolate syrup, and finish with a veritable snowstorm of malted milk powder; there you have it. You can also use the Double Chocolate variation on the Vanilla Buttercream Frosting (pages 150 and 151) in place of the Malted Milk variation for a chocolate malted flavor.

*serves*
**12 to 16**

## cake

½ cup (4 oz/113 g) **whole milk**

5 tablespoons (2½ oz/71 g) **unsalted butter**, cut into pieces

2 teaspoons **pure vanilla extract**

1¾ cups (7⅞ oz/223 g) **unbleached all-purpose flour**

3 tablespoons **malted milk powder**

1 tablespoon **baking powder**

1 teaspoon **table salt**

7 large **eggs**, at room temperature

1⅔ cups (11⅝ oz/329 g) **granulated sugar**

## assembly and serving

**Classic Soak** (Chocolate variation; page 156)

**Vanilla Buttercream Frosting** (full recipe, Malted Milk variation; pages 150 and 151)

**Bittersweet Chocolate Glaze or Sauce** (page 157), warmed

3 tablespoons **malted milk powder**

### BAKE THE CAKE

**1.** Position a rack in the center of the oven and preheat the oven to 350°F (180°C/gas mark 4). Lightly grease and flour the bottom and sides of the half-sheet pan.

**2.** In a small saucepan over medium-low heat, or in a heatproof container in the microwave for 15 second increments, heat the milk and butter together until the butter is melted and the mixture is very hot but not boiling. Stir in the vanilla.

**3.** Combine the flour, malted milk powder, baking powder, and salt in a medium bowl and whisk until blended. In the bowl of a stand mixer fitted with the whisk attachment, beat the eggs on medium-high speed until pale and foamy, about 3 minutes. Gradually add the sugar and continue beating until a ribbon of batter falls from the beater when lifted, about 3 more minutes.

**4.** With the mixer on medium-low speed, gradually add the flour mixture and mix until just blended, about 15 seconds. With the mixer running, gradually add the hot milk mixture and mix until just blended, about 15 seconds.

**5.** Scrape the batter into the prepared pan and, using an offset spatula, spread evenly. Bake until a toothpick inserted in the center comes out clean, 15 to 17 minutes.

**6.** Let the cake cool in the pan.

### ASSEMBLE AND SERVE THE CAKE

**7.** Spread the soak and then the frosting evenly over the cake layer. Follow the directions for storing and serving the cake (see page 21).

**8.** Just before serving, drizzle some of the glaze on top of the cake and sprinkle with the malted milk powder. Slice and serve with additional warm glaze.

THIS CHARMING CAKE WAS INSPIRED by a small batch of mini muffins that I make for my daughter when she's home for a visit. The texture is light and the flavor is deeply vanilla, while the mini chips offer the perfect burst of chocolate flavor. I've paired the cake with a similar-flavored whipped cream, but you can also serve it as is or bake it with the sugar topping used in the Peach-Studded Cream Cheese Pound Cake (page 31).

## cake

4 cups (18 oz/511 g) **unbleached all-purpose flour**

2½ teaspoons **baking powder**

2 teaspoons **table salt**

¼ teaspoon **baking soda**

2½ sticks (1 cup plus 4 tablespoons/10 oz/283 g) **unsalted butter**, softened

2 tablespoons **neutral oil**

2 cups (14 oz/397 g) **granulated sugar**

4 large **eggs**, at room temperature

4 teaspoons **pure vanilla extract**

1⅔ cups (13¼ oz/376 g) **whole milk**, at room temperature

1 cup (6 oz/170 g) finely chopped **bittersweet chocolate** or **mini chips**

## assembly and serving

**Vanilla Mascarpone Cream Frosting** (full recipe, with Chocolate Chips add-in; pages 145 and 153)

**Chocolate Curls** (page 163)

## flavor swap

**WHITE CHOCOLATE**
Use an equal amount of chopped white chocolate in place of the bittersweet in the batter.

### BAKE THE CAKE

**1.** Position a rack in the center of the oven and preheat the oven to 350°F (180°C/gas mark 4). Lightly grease and flour the bottom and sides of the half-sheet pan.

**2.** Combine the flour, baking powder, salt, and baking soda in a medium bowl and whisk until blended. In the bowl of a stand mixer fitted with the paddle attachment, beat the butter and oil on medium speed until smooth, about 1 minute. Add the sugar and continue beating on medium-high speed until fluffy and lighter in color, 2 to 3 more minutes.

**3.** Add 3 of the eggs, one at a time, beating until blended after each addition. Add the vanilla along with the remaining egg. Add one-third of the flour mixture and mix on low speed until just blended, about 30 seconds. Add half the milk and mix until just blended, about 30 seconds more. Add another third of the flour mixture and mix on low speed until just blended, about 30 seconds. Add the remaining milk and mix until just blended, about 30 seconds. Add the remaining flour mixture and the chocolate and mix until just blended, about 30 seconds.

**4.** Scrape the batter into the prepared pan and, using an offset spatula, spread it evenly. Bake until a toothpick inserted in the center comes out clean, 20 to 22 minutes.

**5.** Let the cake cool in the pan.

### ASSEMBLE AND SERVE THE CAKE

**6.** Spread the frosting evenly over the cake layer. Follow the directions for storing and serving the cake (see page 21).

**7.** Just before serving, scatter the chocolate curls on top of the cake, if using.

*serves*
**12 to 16**

**THE NOT-SO SECRET TO THE STUNNING COLOR** of this cake is food coloring! I prefer using gel coloring–a little goes a long way–but a double dose of the liquid variety will do as well. I've added a twist to the cake's cream cheese frosting. Folding in some crushed crisp chocolate cookies lends flavor as well as a fun texture to the classic topping.

serves
**12 to 16**

### cake

½ cup (4 oz/113 g) **whole milk**

5 tablespoons (2½ oz/71 g) **unsalted butter,** cut into pieces

2 teaspoons **pure vanilla extract**

1 teaspoon **red food coloring gel**

1½ cups (6¾ oz/191 g) **unbleached all-purpose flour**

⅓ cup (1 oz/27 g) **unsweetened natural cocoa powder,** sifted

1 tablespoon **baking powder**

1 teaspoon **table salt**

7 large **eggs,** at room temperature

1⅔ cups (11⅝ oz/329 g) **granulated sugar**

### assembly and serving

**Classic Soak** (Cream variation; page 156)

**Vanilla Cream Cheese Frosting** (full recipe, with Cookie Crumbs add-in using chocolate cookies; pages 139 and 153)

½ cup ground (2½ oz/71 g) **chocolate cookies** (optional)

### BAKE THE CAKE

**1.** Position a rack in the center of the oven and preheat the oven to 350°F (180°C/gas mark 4). Lightly grease and flour the bottom and sides of the half-sheet pan.

**2.** In a small saucepan over medium-low heat, or in a heatproof container in the microwave for 15-second increments, heat the milk and butter together until the butter is melted and the mixture is very hot but not boiling. Stir in the vanilla and the food coloring.

**3.** Combine the flour, cocoa, baking powder, and salt in a medium bowl and whisk until blended. In the bowl of a stand mixer fitted with the whisk attachment, beat the eggs on medium-high speed until pale and foamy, about 3 minutes. Gradually add the sugar and continue beating until a ribbon of batter falls from the beater when lifted, about 3 more minutes.

**4.** With the mixer on medium-low speed, gradually add the flour mixture and mix until just blended, about 15 seconds. With the mixer running, gradually add the hot milk mixture and mix until just blended, about 15 seconds.

**5.** Scrape the batter into the prepared pan and, using an offset spatula, spread evenly. Bake until a toothpick inserted in the center comes out clean, 15 to 17 minutes.

**6.** Let the cake cool in the pan.

### ASSEMBLE AND SERVE THE CAKE

**7.** Spread the soak and then the frosting evenly over the cake layer. Follow the directions for storing and serving the cake (see page 21). Just before serving, scatter cookie crumbs over the top of the cake, if desired.

### flavor swap

**VANILLA** Use the Vanilla Mascarpone Cream Frosting (full recipe, page 145) in place of the cream cheese frosting and fold in the crushed cookies.

**WARM SPICES PAIRED WITH A BURST** of fresh, sweet mango flavors (puree and slices), buttery macadamia nuts, and big flakes of crunchy coconut turn this cake into a tropical daydream! I keep batches of crushed mango in my freezer so I can whip up this lovely cake any time I'm craving a taste of the tropics.

As lovers of chai tea know, blends vary in spice and intensity, so use your personal favorite. If you want to ramp up the spicy goodness in your cake, include the optional cinnamon and cardamom.

## cake

⅔ cup (5⅝ oz/159 g) **coconut milk**

1 tea bag **unsweetened chai tea**

5 tablespoons (2½ oz/71 g) **unsalted butter**

1½ teaspoons **pure vanilla extract**

1¾ cups (7⅞ oz/223 g) **unbleached all-purpose flour**

1 tablespoon **baking powder**

1 teaspoon **table salt**

¾ teaspoon **ground cinnamon** (optional)

¼ teaspoon **ground cardamom** (optional)

7 large **eggs**, at room temperature

1 cup (7 oz/198 g) **granulated sugar**

⅔ cup (4⅝ oz/131 g) packed **light brown sugar**

*ingredients continued*

### BAKE THE CAKE

**1.** Position a rack in the center of the oven and preheat the oven to 350°F (180°C/gas mark 4). Lightly grease and flour the bottom and sides of the half-sheet pan.

**2.** In a small saucepan over medium-low heat, or in a heatproof container in the microwave for 15-second increments, heat the coconut milk until very hot but not boiling. Add the tea bag, cover with a small plate, and let steep at least 15 minutes or up to 1 hour. Remove the tea bag and squeeze out all the liquid. You should have ½ cup (4 oz/113 g). Add the butter and vanilla and stir until the butter is melted, reheating the milk if necessary.

**3.** Combine the flour, baking powder, salt, and cinnamon and cardamom if using, in a medium bowl and whisk until blended. In the bowl of a stand mixer fitted with the whisk attachment, beat the eggs on medium-high speed until pale and foamy, about 3 minutes. Gradually add the sugars and continue beating until a ribbon of batter falls from the beater when lifted, about 3 more minutes.

**4.** With the mixer on medium-low speed, gradually add the flour mixture and mix until just blended, about 15 seconds. With the mixer running, gradually add the hot milk mixture and mix until just blended, about 15 seconds.

**5.** Scrape the batter into the prepared pan and, using an offset spatula, spread evenly. Bake until a toothpick inserted in the center comes out clean, 15 to 17 minutes.

**6.** Let the cake cool in the pan.

*serves*
**12 to 16**

*continued*

## assembly and serving

½ cup (5½ oz/156 g) **mango jam**

**Vanilla Mascarpone Cream Frosting** (full recipe, with Crushed Fruit add-in using fresh mango; pages 145 and 153)

Fresh **mango** pieces (see sidebar; optional)

**Macadamia nuts**, toasted and roughly chopped (optional)

**Unsweetened flaked coconut**, toasted or untoasted (optional)

## ASSEMBLE AND SERVE THE CAKE

**7.** Spread the jam and then the frosting evenly over the cake layer. Follow the directions for storing and serving the cake (see page 21).

**8.** Just before serving, scatter the mango, macadamia nuts, and coconut on top of the cake, if desired.

### flavor swap

**HONEY CREAM CHEESE**  Omit the jam and use the Vanilla Cream Cheese Frosting (full recipe, Honey variation; page 139) in place of the mascarpone cream.

## CHOOSING AND CUTTING MANGOS

For the best results, select mangos that give slightly when you press gently near the stem end with your thumb. They should be free of bruises and blemishes and have a spicy-citrus fragrance.

To remove the flesh, arrange the mango sideways on the cutting board with the flatter side down. Position a sharp knife just off center and cut down one side, avoiding the pit. Repeat with the other side. Lay the mango flat and slice around the pit to cut away the flesh. Arrange one half, skin side down, on the cutting board and, using a paring knife, cut a small or large crosshatch pattern in the flesh. Be careful you don't cut all the way through the skin. Using your fingers, push the mango inside out so the flesh pops up and cut it away from the skin.

**WHEN I MOVED BACK TO THE UNITED STATES** from Paris (many years ago), one of the first things I baked for my family and friends was a version of this cake. Its color is stunning and the flavor is fresh and bright. In fact, it's just the thing to brighten a New England winter day. I've garnished this version with sliced strawberries and chopped pistachios (for maximum appeal, make sure they are vibrantly colored), but you can also serve it with a mixture of blueberries, raspberries, and cherries.

## cake

4 large **eggs**, separated, at room temperature

1¼ cups (8¾ oz/248 g) **granulated sugar**

1⅓ cups (6 oz/170 g) **unbleached all-purpose flour**

1½ teaspoons **baking powder**

1 teaspoon **table salt**

⅔ cup (5⅜ oz/152 g) **buttermilk**, at room temperature

6 tablespoons (2⅞ oz/82 g) **neutral oil**

2 teaspoons fresh **lemon juice**

1 teaspoon finely grated **lemon zest**

## strawberry mousse

¼ cup (2 oz/57 g) fresh **lemon juice**, or more as needed

2 tablespoons **water**

1 envelope (¼ oz/7 g) **unflavored powdered gelatin**

½ cup (3½ oz/99 g) **granulated sugar**

1 teaspoon finely grated **lemon zest**, or more as needed

Pinch of **table salt**

*ingredients continued*

## BAKE THE CAKE

**1.** Position a rack in the center of the oven and preheat the oven to 350°F (180°C/gas mark 4). Lightly grease and flour the bottom and sides of the half-sheet pan.

**2.** In the bowl of a stand mixer fitted with the whisk attachment, beat the egg whites on medium-low speed until foamy, 1 to 2 minutes. Increase the speed to medium and beat until the whites form very soft peaks. Continue beating while slowly adding ¼ cup (1¾ oz/50 g) of the sugar. Beat until the whites are thick, shiny, and form medium-firm peaks, 2 to 4 more minutes. Scrape the whites into a medium bowl and wipe out the mixer bowl.

**3.** Put the flour into the mixer bowl and add the remaining 1 cup (7 oz/198 g) sugar, the egg yolks, the baking powder, salt, buttermilk, oil, lemon juice, and lemon zest. Mix with the paddle attachment on low speed until blended, about 15 seconds. Increase the speed to medium high and beat until the mixture is well blended, 1 to 2 more minutes.

**4.** Scrape about one-fourth of the whites into the flour mixture and, using a rubber spatula, gently stir until blended. Add the remaining whites and gently fold in until just blended with no visible streaks of the whites.

**5.** Scrape the batter into the prepared pan and, using an offset spatula, spread evenly. Bake until a toothpick inserted in the center comes out clean, 13 to 15 minutes.

**6.** Let the cake cool in the pan.

*serves*
**12 to 16**

*continued*

2 cups (16 oz/454 g) **strawberry puree**

2 large **egg whites**, at room temperature

¼ teaspoon **cream of tartar**

⅔ cup (5⅝ oz/159 g) **heavy cream**, chilled

### *assembly and serving*

½ cup (5½ oz/156 g) **strawberry jam**

Handful of sliced fresh **strawberries** (optional)

Handful of chopped **pistachios** (optional)

### *flavor swap*

**BLUEBERRY** · Use the same amount of pureed blueberries in place of the strawberry puree in the mousse. Use blueberry jam in place of the strawberry jam.

## MAKE THE STRAWERRY MOUSSE

**7.** In a large microwave-safe bowl, combine the lemon juice and water and sprinkle the gelatin evenly over the top. Set aside to soften, 1 to 3 minutes. Once the gelatin has absorbed the liquid and is plump, microwave in short pulses until it is completely melted and clear, 30 to 60 seconds.

**8.** Add ¼ cup (1¾ oz/50 g) of the granulated sugar, the lemon zest, and salt and stir the mixture until the sugar is dissolved, 1 to 2 minutes. Briefly reheat, if necessary. Add the strawberry puree and whisk until very well blended, 2 to 3 minutes. Taste and add a little more lemon juice and zest, if necessary. The flavor should be vibrant.

**9.** Refrigerate, stirring frequently, until the mixture is cooled and thickened, 15 to 30 minutes (see Note). It should fall from the spatula like gelatinous, unbeaten egg whites and mound slightly. (For faster cooling, set the bowl over a larger bowl filled with ice and a little water, stirring and scraping the sides frequently.)

**10.** In the bowl of a stand mixer fitted with the whisk attachment, combine the egg whites and cream of tartar and beat on medium speed until frothy, 30 to 45 seconds. Increase the speed to medium high and beat until soft peaks form, 1 to 2 minutes more. Continue beating while gradually adding the remaining ¼ cup (1¾ oz/50 g) sugar, stopping occasionally to scrape down the sides of the bowl. Beat until the whites form firm and glossy peaks when the beaters are lifted, 1 to 3 minutes.

**11.** Scrape the whites into a medium bowl and wipe out the inside of the bowl. Add the cream and beat on medium speed until firm peaks form when the beaters are lifted, 2 to 3 minutes. Scrape the whipped cream into the chilled strawberry mixture and, using a spatula, fold in until blended. Add about one-fourth of the egg whites and gently stir until blended. Add the remaining whites and gently fold in until just blended.

## ASSEMBLE AND SERVE THE CAKE

**12.** Spread the strawberry jam evenly over the cake layer. Spread the mousse over the jam evenly. Refrigerate for 1 hour, then cover loosely and continue to chill until set and very firm, at least 8 hours or up to 24 hours.

**13.** Just before serving, scatter the strawberries and pistachios on top of the cake, if desired.

**NOTE:** If the gelatin-puree mixture is overchilled and too thick, the cream and whites won't incorporate easily and you'll end up with a lumpy mousse. Before adding the beaten cream and whites, heat the gelatin-puree mixture gently in the microwave in short pulses until it becomes more liquid, whisk until smooth then repeat the chilling process.

**IT'S NO SURPRISE THAT PEANUT BUTTER AND MARSHMALLOW** make excellent sandwich partners, so it's not a huge leap to partner them in a cake. The end results are a more grown-up look and more subtle flavor, but every bite will remind you of that childhood staple.

## cake

4 large **eggs**, separated, at room temperature

¼ cup (1¾ oz/50 g) **granulated sugar**

1½ cups (6 oz/170 g) **cake flour**

¾ cup (5¼ oz/149 g) packed **light brown sugar**

2 teaspoons **baking powder**

½ teaspoon **table salt**

⅓ cup (3 oz/85 g) **creamy peanut butter**

½ cup (3⅞ oz/110 g) **neutral oil**

½ cup (4 oz/113 g) **whole milk**, at room temperature

1½ teaspoons **pure vanilla extract**

## assembly and serving

**Vanilla Marshmallow Frosting** (full recipe, page 142)

Handful of chopped lightly salted **peanuts** (optional)

## flavor swap

**DOUBLE PEANUT BUTTER**
Use the Vanilla Cream Cheese Frosting (full recipe, Peanut Butter variation; page 139) in place of the marshmallow frosting.

### BAKE THE CAKE

**1.** Position a rack in the center of the oven and preheat the oven to 350°F (180°C/gas mark 4). Lightly grease and flour the bottom and sides of the half-sheet pan.

**2.** In the bowl of a stand mixer fitted with the whisk attachment, beat the egg whites on medium-low speed until foamy, 1 to 2 minutes. Increase the speed to medium, and beat until the whites form soft peaks, 1 to 2 minutes. Continue beating while slowly adding the granulated sugar. Beat until the whites are thick, shiny, and form medium-firm peaks, 2 to 4 minutes. Scrape the whites into a medium bowl and wipe out the inside of the bowl.

**3.** Sift the flour into the mixer bowl, and add the brown sugar, the egg yolks, the baking powder, salt, peanut butter, oil, milk, and vanilla. Mix with the paddle attachment on medium-low speed until blended, about 15 seconds. Increase the speed to medium high and beat until the mixture is well blended, 1 to 2 minutes.

**4.** Scrape about one-fourth of the whites into the flour mixture and, using a rubber spatula, gently stir until blended. Add the remaining whites and gently fold in until just blended with no visible streaks of the whites.

**5.** Scrape the batter into the prepared pan and, using an offset spatula, spread evenly. Bake until the top springs back when lightly touched, 17 to 19 minutes.

**6.** Let the cake cool in the pan.

### ASSEMBLE AND SERVE THE CAKE

**7.** Spread the frosting evenly over the cake layer. Follow the directions for storing and serving the cake (see page 21).

**8.** Just before serving, scatter the peanuts on top of the cake, if desired.

*serves*
**12 to 16**

A GOOD CRUMB-TOPPED CAKE has long been one of my favorite breakfast treats. For me, this cake is all about the top layer of crumbs, so for this sheet-pan version of the classic, I've doubled the crumb layer and paired it with a vanilla cake base that is just as scrumptious.

## crumb topping

3 cups (13½ oz/383 g) **unbleached all-purpose flour**

2⅔ cups (18⅝ oz/528 g) firmly packed **dark brown sugar**

2 tablespoons **ground cinnamon**

½ teaspoon **table salt**

2 sticks (1 cup/8 oz/227 g) **unsalted butter**, melted

¼ cup (1⅞ oz/53 g) **neutral oil**

## cake

4 cups (18 oz/511 g) **unbleached all-purpose flour**

5 teaspoons **baking powder**

1 teaspoon **table salt**

2 sticks (1 cup/8 oz/227 g) **unsalted butter**, softened

1½ cups (10½ oz/298 g) **granulated sugar**

4 large **eggs**, at room temperature

4 teaspoons **pure vanilla extract**

1⅓ cups (11⅓ oz/322 g) **buttermilk**, at room temperature

**MAKE THE CRUMB TOPPING**

**1.** Combine the flour, brown sugar, cinnamon, and salt in a medium bowl and mix with a fork until well blended. Add the butter and oil and mix until well blended. Spread out on a sheet pan and refrigerate until well chilled, about 20 minutes.

**BAKE THE CAKE**

**2.** Position a rack in the center of the oven and preheat the oven to 350°F (180°C/gas mark 4). Lightly grease and flour the bottom and sides of the half-sheet pan.

**3.** Combine the flour, baking powder, and salt in a medium bowl and whisk until blended. In the bowl of a stand mixer fitted with the paddle attachment, add the butter and beat on medium speed until smooth, about 1 minute. Add the sugar and continue beating on medium-high speed until fluffy and lighter in color, 2 to 3 minutes.

**4.** Add 3 of the eggs, one at a time, beating until blended after each addition. Add the vanilla along with the remaining egg. Add one-third of the flour mixture and mix on low speed until just blended, about 30 seconds. Add half the buttermilk and mix until just blended, about 30 seconds. Add another third of the flour mixture and mix on low speed until just blended, about 30 seconds. Add the remaining buttermilk and mix until just blended, about 30 seconds. Add the remaining flour mixture and mix until just blended, about 30 seconds.

**5.** Scrape the batter into the prepared pan and, using an offset spatula, spread evenly. Break up any very large pieces of the topping and sprinkle over the batter. Bake until a toothpick inserted in the center comes out clean, 32 to 34 minutes.

**6.** Let the cake cool in the pan.

**7.** Slice and serve, or cover and store at room temperature for up to 4 days.

**IF YOU ARE A PUMPKIN PIE FAN,** you will love this cake. The cake layer has the warm, spicy flavors and the creamy frosting adds the richness of a pie but without the crust. It's a tasty ending to any winter meal.

A note about organic canned pumpkin puree: As it tends to be thinner than the standard store-bought variety, drain off any water beforehand. To do so, set a fine-mesh sieve over a small bowl and line the inside with two layers of cheesecloth or paper towels. Scrape the puree into the sieve and let it drain for about 2 hours before proceeding with the recipe.

*serves*
**12 to 16**

## cake

6 large **eggs**, separated, at room temperature

1¼ cups (8¾ oz/248 g) packed **dark brown sugar**

2 cups (9 oz/255 g) **unbleached all-purpose flour**

3¾ teaspoons **ground cinnamon**

2½ teaspoons **baking powder**

1½ teaspoons **ground ginger**

1 teaspoon **table salt**

½ teaspoon **ground nutmeg**

¾ cup (6 oz/170 g) canned unsweetened **pumpkin puree**, at room temperature

⅔ cup (5⅛ oz/145 g) **neutral oil**

2 teaspoons **pure vanilla extract**

### BAKE THE CAKE

**1.** Position a rack in the center of the oven and preheat the oven to 350°F (180°C/gas mark 4). Lightly grease and flour the bottom and sides of the half-sheet pan.

**2.** In the bowl of a stand mixer fitted with the whisk attachment, beat the egg whites on medium-low speed until foamy, about 1 minute. Increase the speed to medium and beat until the whites form soft peaks, 1 to 2 minutes. Continue beating while slowly adding ½ cup (3½ oz/99 g) of the brown sugar. Beat until the whites are thick, shiny, and form medium-firm peaks, 2 to 3 more minutes. Scrape the whites into a medium bowl and wipe out the mixer bowl.

**3.** Sift the flour into the mixer bowl, add the remaining ¾ cup (5¼ oz/149 g) brown sugar, the cinnamon, baking powder, ginger, salt, and nutmeg. Add the egg yolks, the pumpkin, oil, and vanilla and mix with the paddle attachment on medium-low speed until blended, about 15 seconds. Increase the speed to medium high and beat until the mixture is well blended, 1 to 2 more minutes.

**4.** Scrape about one-fourth of the whites into the flour mixture and, using a rubber spatula, gently stir until blended. Add the remaining whites and gently fold in until just blended, with no visible streaks of the whites.

**5.** Scrape the batter into the prepared pan and, using an offset spatula, spread evenly. Bake until a toothpick inserted in the center comes out clean, 17 to 19 minutes.

**6.** Let the cake cool in the pan.

## assembly and serving

**Vanilla Cream Cheese Frosting** (full recipe, with Cookie Crumbs add-in using ginger cookies; pages 139 and 153)

Finely chopped **crystallized ginger**, for garnish (optional)

### ASSEMBLE AND SERVE THE CAKE

**7.** Spread the frosting evenly over the cake layer. Follow the directions for storing and serving the cake (see page 21).

**8.** Just before serving, scatter the ginger on top of the cake, if desired.

### flavor swaps

**COCONUT BUTTERCREAM** Use the Vanilla Buttercream Frosting (full recipe, Coconut variation; pages 150 and 151) in place of the cream cheese frosting and fold in the cookie crumbs.

**ORANGE MASCARPONE CREAM** Use the Vanilla Mascarpone Cream Frosting (full recipe, with Citrus add-in using orange zest; pages 145 and 153) in place of the cream cheese frosting. Garnish with orange supremes (see Note on page 52), if desired.

# NUTTY CHOCOLATE UPSIDE-DOWNER

**FOLKS USUALLY EQUATE AN UPSIDE-DOWN CAKE** with a fruit topping, but a caramelly nut topping and moist chocolate layer is equally delicious.

serves
**12 to 16**

## caramel

1½ cups (10½ oz/298 g) packed **dark brown sugar**

1¼ sticks (½ cup plus 2 tablespoons/5 oz/ 142 g) **unsalted butter**

6 tablespoons (3 oz/ 85 g) **water**

2⅔ cups (13⅜ oz/379 g) **walnuts**, toasted and roughly chopped

## cake

⅔ cup (12 oz/340 g) **unbleached all-purpose flour**

1 cup (3 oz/85 g) **unsweetened natural cocoa powder**, sifted

1½ teaspoons **baking powder**

½ teaspoon **baking soda**

½ teaspoon **table salt**

2½ sticks (1 cup plus 4 tablespoons/10 oz/ 283 g) **unsalted butter**, softened

2 cups (14 oz/397 g) **granulated sugar**

6 large **eggs**, at room temperature

2 teaspoons **pure vanilla extract**

1 cup (8½ oz/241 g) **buttermilk**, at room temperature

## flavor swap

**NUTS** · Use any other nut or nut combinations in place of the walnuts.

### MAKE THE CARAMEL

**1.** Have ready an ungreased half-sheet pan. Combine the brown sugar, butter, and water in a medium saucepan. Cook over medium heat, stirring often, until the butter is melted and the mixture is smooth, about 4 minutes. Bring to a boil and pour into the pan, swirling to evenly coat the bottom. Scatter the nuts evenly over the caramel.

### BAKE THE CAKE

**2.** Position a rack in the center of the oven and preheat the oven to 350°F (180°C/gas mark 4).

**3.** Combine the flour, cocoa, baking powder, baking soda, and salt in a medium bowl and whisk until blended. In the bowl of a stand mixer fitted with the paddle attachment, add the butter and beat on medium speed until smooth, about 1 minute. Add the sugar and continue beating on medium-high speed until fluffy and lighter in color, 2 to 3 more minutes.

**4.** Add 5 of the eggs, one at a time, beating until blended after each addition. Add the vanilla along with the remaining egg. Add one-third of the flour mixture and mix on low speed until just blended, about 30 seconds. Add half the buttermilk and mix until just blended, about 30 seconds more. Add another third of the flour mixture and mix on low speed until just blended, about 30 seconds. Add the remaining buttermilk and mix until just blended, about 30 seconds. Add the remaining flour mixture and mix until just blended, about 30 seconds.

**5.** Drop small amounts of the batter over the caramel and nuts and, using an offset spatula, spread evenly. Bake until a toothpick inserted in the center comes out clean, 15 to 17 minutes.

### SERVE THE CAKE

**6.** Immediately run a paring knife around the inside edge of the pan. Set a large cutting board on top of the pan and invert the cake. Let the inverted pan rest, then gently remove the pan and reposition any nuts stuck to the pan onto the cake.

**7.** Slice and serve or cover and store at room temperature for up to 4 days.

**HAVE YOU EVER TASTED ONE OF THOSE CHOCOLATE-ORANGE CANDY BALLS** that, when broken apart into pieces, resemble orange sections? Well, let me tell you, a single bite into one of those sections explodes with bright sunshine-y orange flavor wrapped in a creamy bittersweet chocolate hug. Hyperbole? Maybe a little, but I assure you that the chocolate-orange flavor combo is *that* good, and while I don't like to brag, I will say that this cake packs that same flavor, presented in a sumptuous sheet cake.

## cake

6 large **eggs**, separated, at room temperature

1 large **egg white**, at room temperature

1¾ cups (12¼ oz/350 g) **granulated sugar**

1½ cups (6 oz/170 g) **cake flour**

⅔ cup (2 oz/57 g) **unsweetened natural cocoa powder**

2 teaspoons **baking powder**

¾ teaspoon **table salt**

4 oz (113 g) **bittersweet chocolate**, melted and cooled slightly

½ cup (3⅞ oz/110 g) **neutral oil**

½ cup (4¼ oz/120 g) **buttermilk**, at room temperature

1 tablespoon finely grated **orange zest**

2 teaspoons **pure vanilla extract**

## assembly and serving

**Classic Soak** (Cream or Citrus variation, using orange; page 156; optional)

**Vanilla Buttercream Frosting** (full recipe, with Citrus add-in using orange zest; pages 150 and 153)

**Orange supremes** (see Note; optional)

### BAKE THE CAKE

**1.** Position a rack in the center of the oven and preheat the oven to 350°F (180°C/gas mark 4). Lightly grease and flour the bottom and sides of the half-sheet pan.

**2.** In the bowl of a stand mixer fitted with the whisk attachment, beat the egg whites on medium-low speed until foamy, about 1 minute. Increase the speed to medium and beat until the whites form soft peaks, 1 to 2 minutes. Continue beating while slowly adding ½ cup (3½ oz/99 g) of the sugar. Beat until the whites are thick, shiny, and form medium-firm peaks, 2 to 3 more minutes. Scrape the whites into a medium bowl and wipe out the mixer bowl.

**3.** Sift the flour and cocoa into the mixer bowl, add the remaining 1¼ cups (8¾ oz/248 g) sugar, the egg yolks, the baking powder, salt, chocolate, oil, buttermilk, orange zest, and vanilla, and mix with the paddle attachment on low speed until just blended, about 15 seconds. Increase the speed to medium high and beat until the mixture is well blended, 1 to 2 minutes.

**4.** Scrape about one-fourth of the whites into the flour mixture and, using a rubber spatula, gently stir until blended. Add the remaining whites and gently fold in until just blended with no visible streaks of the whites.

**5.** Scrape the batter into the prepared pan and, using an offset spatula, spread evenly. Bake until a toothpick inserted in the center comes out clean, 16 to 18 minutes.

**6.** Let the cake cool in the pan.

*serves*
**12 *to* 16**

*continued*

## ASSEMBLE AND SERVE THE CAKE

**7.** Brush the soak, if using, evenly over the cake layer and spread on the frosting.

**8.** Follow the directions for storing and serving the cake (see page 21).

**9.** Just before serving, scatter the orange supremes on top of the cake, if desired.

**NOTE:** For orange supremes (sections), slice off the ends of an orange with a sharp knife. Stand the fruit on one cut end on a cutting board and slice off the skin following the curve of the fruit to remove all the white pith without sacrificing too much flesh. Working over a bowl, hold the fruit in one hand and, using the membranes as a guide, cut the segments free, allowing them to fall into the bowl. Repeat with additional oranges, if desired. Drain the segments before serving.

*flavor swaps*

**DOUBLE-STUFFED OREO** · Use the Vanilla Buttercream Frosting (full recipe, with Cookie Crumbs add-in using cream-filled chocolate cookies; pages 150 and 153) in place of the orange-flavored buttercream and omit the orange zest in the cake batter. Top with coarsely chopped cream-filled chocolate cookies in place of the orange supremes.

**RASPBERRY** · Use the Vanilla Mascarpone Cream Frosting (full recipe, Jammin' variation using raspberry jam; pages 145 and 146) in place of the orange-flavored buttercream. Top with fresh raspberries in place of the orange supremes.

WHEN I WAS GROWING UP, SPICE CAKES were a mystery to me. We never had them at home, but I had a friend who requested one for her birthday every year. The flavor reminds me of a snickerdoodle cookie with frosting on top.

## cake

2½ cups (12 oz/340 g) **unbleached all-purpose flour**

1¾ teaspoons **baking powder**

¼ teaspoon **baking soda**

1¾ teaspoons **ground cinnamon**

1¼ teaspoons **ground ginger**

½ teaspoon **ground nutmeg**

¾ teaspoon **table salt**

2 sticks (1 cup/8 oz/227 g) **unsalted butter**, softened

1 cup (7 oz/198 g) **granulated sugar**

¾ cup (5¼ oz/149 g) packed **light brown sugar**

4 large **eggs**, at room temperature

2 teaspoons **pure vanilla extract**

1¼ cups (10⅝ oz/301 g) **buttermilk**, at room temperature

## assembly and serving

**Vanilla Buttercream Frosting** (full recipe, Nut variation using walnuts; pages 150 and 152)

1 cup (4 oz/113 g) chopped **walnuts**, toasted (optional)

## BAKE THE CAKE

**1.** Position a rack in the center of the oven and preheat the oven to 350°F (180°C/gas mark 4). Lightly grease and flour the bottom and sides of the half-sheet pan.

**2.** Combine the flour, baking powder, baking soda, cinnamon, ginger, nutmeg, and salt in a medium bowl and whisk until blended.

**3.** In the bowl of a stand mixer fitted with the paddle attachment, beat the butter on medium speed until smooth, about 1 minute. Add the granulated and brown sugars and continue beating on medium-high speed until fluffy and lighter in color, 2 to 3 more minutes.

**4.** Add 3 of the eggs, one at a time, beating until blended after each addition. Add the vanilla along with the remaining egg. Add one-third of the flour mixture and mix on low speed until just blended, about 30 seconds. Add half the buttermilk and mix until just blended, about 30 seconds more. Add another third of the flour mixture and mix on low speed until just blended, about 30 seconds. Add the remaining buttermilk and mix until just blended, about 30 seconds. Add the remaining flour mixture and mix until just blended, about 30 seconds.

**5.** Scrape the batter into the prepared pan and, using an offset spatula, spread evenly. Bake until the top springs back when lightly touched, 20 to 22 minutes.

**6.** Let the cake cool in the pan.

## ASSEMBLE AND SERVE THE CAKE

**7.** Spread the frosting evenly over the cake layer. Follow the directions for storing and serving the cake (see page 21).

**8.** Just before serving, scatter the walnuts on top of the cake, if desired.

### flavor swap

**HONEY-SPICED**   Use the Vanilla Cream Cheese Frosting (full recipe, Brown Sugar variation; page 139) in place of the walnut-flavored buttercream.

*serves* **12 *to* 16**

**CHIFFON CAKES ARE KNOWN FOR THEIR LIGHT AND SPONGY TEXTURE.**
Adding a creamy hazelnut spread to the mix increases the moisture and adds a big punch of flavor. For a double dose of hazelnut flavor, I like to top the cake with a hazelnut variation on the mascarpone frosting.

*serves*
**12 to 16**

## cake

6 large **eggs**, separated, at room temperature

1¼ cups (8¾ oz/248 g) **granulated sugar**

2¼ cups (9 oz/255 g) **cake flour**

1 tablespoon **baking powder**

¾ teaspoon **table salt**

¾ cup (7½ oz/213 g) **hazelnut spread**, such as Nutella

⅔ cup (5⅛ oz/145 g) **neutral oil**

½ cup (4¼ oz/120 g) **buttermilk**, at room temperature

1½ teaspoons **pure vanilla extract**

## assembly and serving

**Vanilla Mascarpone Cream Frosting** (full recipe, Nutella variation, with Nuts add-in using hazelnuts; pages 145 and 153)

Toasted chopped **hazelnuts**, for garnish

**Unsweetened natural cocoa powder**, for dusting

### flavor swap

**CINNAMON HAZELNUT**
Use Vanilla Buttercream Frosting (full recipe, with Cookie Crumbs add-in using cinnamon graham crackers; pages 150 and 153) in place of the mascarpone cream.

### BAKE THE CAKE

**1.** Position a rack in the center of the oven and preheat the oven to 350°F (180°C/gas mark 4). Lightly grease and flour the bottom and sides of the half-sheet pan.

**2.** In the bowl of a stand mixer fitted with the whisk attachment, beat the egg whites on medium-low speed until foamy, 1 to 2 minutes. Increase the speed to medium and beat until the whites form soft peaks. Continue beating while slowly adding ½ cup (3½ ounces/99 grams) of the sugar. Beat until the whites are thick, shiny, and form medium-firm peaks, 2 to 4 more minutes. Scrape the whites into a medium bowl and wipe out the mixer bowl.

**3.** Sift the flour into the mixer bowl and add the remaining ¾ cup (5¼ oz/149 g) sugar, the baking powder, salt, egg yolks, hazelnut spread, oil, buttermilk, and vanilla. Mix with the paddle attachment on low speed until blended, about 30 seconds. Increase the speed to medium high and beat until the mixture is well blended, 1 to 2 minutes.

**4.** Scrape about one-fourth of the whites into the flour mixture and, using a rubber spatula, gently stir until blended. Add the remaining whites and gently fold in until just blended with no visible streaks of the whites.

**5.** Scrape the batter into the prepared pan and, using an offset spatula, spread evenly. Bake until a toothpick inserted in the center comes out clean, 17 to 19 minutes.

**6.** Let the cake cool in the pan.

### ASSEMBLE AND SERVE THE CAKE

**7.** Spread the frosting evenly over the cake layer. Follow the directions for storing and serving the cake (see page 21).

**8.** Just before serving, scatter the hazelnuts and a dusting of cocoa powder over the top, if desired.

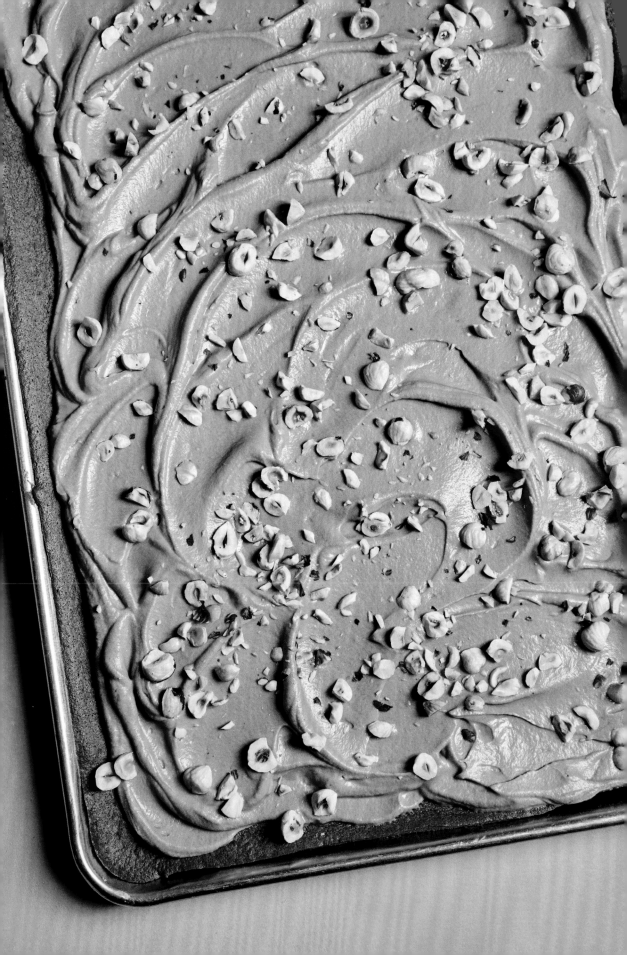

**IN 1852, THE AMERICAN BAKER SAMUEL GERMAN** (hence the apostrophe in German's) created a dark baking chocolate for the Baker's Chocolate Company and developed an iconic layer cake along with it. This sheet-pan version of the classic cake features the same light and airy texture paired with a thick and sweet coconut-and-nut topping.

Oh, and don't forget to mark your calendars; June 11 is National German's Chocolate Cake Day!

*serves*
**12 to 16**

## *cake*

3 ounces (85 g) **semisweet chocolate**, finely chopped

2 tablespoons **unsweetened natural cocoa powder**

⅓ cup (2⅝ oz/74 g) **water**

2 cups (9 oz/255 g) **unbleached all-purpose flour**

1 teaspoon **baking soda**

¾ teaspoon **table salt**

1 stick (½ cup/4 oz/113 g) **unsalted butter**, softened

1 cup (7 oz/198 g) packed **light brown sugar**

⅔ cup (4⅝ oz/131 g) **granulated sugar**

3 large **eggs**, at room temperature

1 large **egg yolk**, at room temperature

1½ teaspoons **pure vanilla extract**

1 cup (8½ oz/241 g) **buttermilk**, at room temperature

## BAKE THE CAKE

**1.** Position a rack in the center of the oven and preheat the oven to 350°F (180°C/gas mark 4). Lightly grease and flour the bottom and sides of the half-sheet pan.

**2.** Combine the chocolate, cocoa, and water in a small heatproof bowl and melt over a pan of simmering water or in a microwave, stirring until smooth and thickened, 2 to 3 minutes. Let cool.

**3.** Combine the flour, baking soda, and salt in a medium bowl and whisk until blended. In the bowl of a stand mixer fitted with the paddle attachment, beat the butter on medium speed until smooth, about 1 minute. Add the brown and granulated sugars and continue beating on medium-high speed until fluffy and lighter in color, 2 to 3 minutes.

**4.** Add 2 of the eggs and the yolk, one at a time, beating until blended after each addition. Add the vanilla along with the remaining egg. Add the chocolate mixture and beat on medium speed until blended, about 30 seconds. Add one-third of the flour mixture and mix on low speed until just blended, about 30 seconds. Add about half the buttermilk and mix until just blended, about 30 seconds. Repeat with the second third of the flour and remaining buttermilk, ending with the final third of the flour mixture.

**5.** Scrape the batter into the prepared pan and, using an offset spatula, spread evenly. Bake until a toothpick inserted in the center comes out clean, 20 to 22 minutes.

**6.** Let the cake cool in the pan.

## coconut-pecan topping

1 can (14 oz/397 g) **sweetened condensed milk**

⅔ cup (4⅝ oz/131 g) packed **light brown sugar**

3 large **egg yolks**, at room temperature

½ stick (4 tablespoons/ 2 oz/57 g) **unsalted butter**, cut into pieces

1½ teaspoons **pure vanilla extract**

¼ teaspoon **table salt**

## assembly and serving

¾ cup (3 oz/85 g) chopped **pecans**, toasted

¾ cup (1⅞ oz/53 g) **sweetened shredded coconut**, toasted

**Bittersweet Chocolate Glaze or Sauce** (page 157), warmed (optional)

### MAKE THE COCONUT-PECAN TOPPING

**7.** Combine the condensed milk, brown sugar, and egg yolks in a medium saucepan and whisk until blended. Add the butter, set over low heat, and cook, whisking constantly, until the butter is melted and the sugar is dissolved, 3 to 5 minutes. Increase the heat to medium low and cook, whisking constantly, until the mixture thickly coats a rubber spatula and a line drawn through it with a finger holds its edges, 3 to 5 minutes. Remove from the heat, stir in the vanilla and salt, and let cool to room temperature, stirring occasionally, 2 to 4 hours. (If not using immediately, cover and refrigerate for up to 2 days. Bring back to room temperature before proceeding.)

### ASSEMBLE AND SERVE THE CAKE

**8.** Drop small dollops of the topping over the cake layer, leaving a 1-inch (2.5 centimeter) border around the edge to minimize spreading. Follow the directions for storing and serving the cake (see page 21).

**9.** Just before serving, scatter the pecans and coconut over the cake. Drizzle with the warm glaze. Slice the cake and serve with a drizzle of chocolate, if desired.

**CINNAMON BUNS ARE ONE OF MY FAVORITE FAMILY TRADITIONS.** This cake version has a swirled vanilla-cinnamon layer covered with a tangy cream cheese frosting, and is topped with toasted pecans and cinnamon chips.

## cake

4 cups (18 oz/511 g) **unbleached all-purpose flour**

2½ teaspoons **baking powder**

2 teaspoons **table salt**

¼ teaspoon **baking soda**

2½ sticks (1 cup plus 4 tablespoons/10 oz/ 283 g) **unsalted butter**, softened

2 tablespoons **neutral oil**

2 cups (14 oz/198 g) **granulated sugar**

4 large **eggs**, at room temperature

4 teaspoons **pure vanilla extract**

1⅔ cups (13½ oz/383 g) **whole milk**, at room temperature

2½ teaspoons **ground cinnamon**

⅓ cup (2 oz/57 g) **cinnamon chips**

## assembly and serving

**Vanilla Cream Cheese Frosting** (full recipe, page 139)

⅔ cup (2⅝ oz/74 g) **pecan halves**, toasted

⅓ cup (2 oz/57 g) **cinnamon chips**

### BAKE THE CAKE

**1.** Position a rack in the center of the oven and preheat the oven to 350°F (180°C/gas mark 4). Lightly grease and flour the bottom and sides of the half-sheet pan.

**2.** Combine the flour, baking powder, salt, and baking soda in a medium bowl and whisk until blended. In the bowl of a stand mixer fitted with the paddle attachment, beat the butter and oil on medium speed until smooth, about 1 minute. Add the sugar and continue beating on medium-high speed until fluffy and lighter in color, 2 to 3 more minutes.

**3.** Add 3 of the eggs, one at a time, beating until blended after each addition. Add the vanilla along with the remaining egg. Add one-third of the flour mixture and mix on low speed until just blended, about 30 seconds. Add half the milk and mix until just blended, about 30 seconds more. Add another third of the flour mixture and mix on low speed until just blended, about 30 seconds. Add the remaining milk and mix until just blended, about 30 seconds. Add the remaining flour mixture and mix until just blended, about 30 seconds.

**4.** Scrape about half of the batter into a medium bowl. Add the cinnamon and cinnamon chips and, using a rubber spatula, fold in until blended. Scrape the vanilla batter into the prepared pan and, using an offset spatula, spread evenly. Using a spoon, dollop the cinnamon batter evenly over the vanilla batter and use the tip of an offset spatula to gently swirl the batters together. Shake the pan gently. Bake until a toothpick inserted in the center comes out clean, 20 to 22 minutes.

**5.** Let the cake cool in the pan.

### ASSEMBLE AND SERVE THE CAKE

**6.** Spread the frosting evenly over the cake layer. Follow the directions for storing and serving the cake (see page 21).

**7.** Just before serving, scatter the pecans and cinnamon chips on top of the cake.

*serves*
**12 to 16**

**THIS CINNAMON-SPIKED APPLE CAKE** is a welcome addition to a picnic or brunch any time of the year. I use crisp, tart apples that retain their shape when baked; Golden Delicious or Mutsu are two great choices, but a local farmers market will have some good local varieties.

This cake, like the Nutty Chocolate Upside-Downer (page 48), is inverted after baking, so you'll need a large cutting board or tray. If that is unavailable or the task feels daunting, simply serve the cake as you would any other classic sheet cake in this chapter.

*serves*
**12 to 16**

## *topping*

1½ cups (10½ oz/298 g) packed **dark brown sugar**

1¼ sticks (½ cup plus 2 tablespoons/5 oz/142 g) **unsalted butter**, cut into pieces

4 or 5 firm **apples** (about 2 pounds/907 g), peeled, cored, and thinly sliced

## *cake*

3 cups (13½ oz/383 g) **unbleached all-purpose flour**

2½ teaspoons **baking powder**

4 teaspoons **ground cinnamon**

1 teaspoon **table salt**

3 sticks (1½ cups/12 oz/ 340 g) **unsalted butter**, softened

1½ cups (10½ oz/298 g) **granulated sugar**

1⅓ cups (9⅜ oz/266 g) packed **dark brown sugar**

6 large **eggs**, at room temperature

1 tablespoon **pure vanilla extract**

1 cup (8 oz/241 g) **whole milk**, at room temperature

### MAKE THE TOPPING

**1.** Have ready an ungreased half-sheet pan. Combine the brown sugar and butter in a medium saucepan. Cook over medium heat, stirring often, until the butter is melted and the mixture is smooth, about 4 minutes. Bring to a boil and pour into the pan, swirling to coat the bottom evenly. Scatter the apple slices evenly over the caramel.

### BAKE THE CAKE

**2.** Position a rack in the center of the oven and preheat the oven to 350°F (180°C/gas mark 4).

**3.** Combine the flour, baking powder, cinnamon, and salt in a medium bowl and whisk until blended. In the bowl of a stand mixer fitted with the paddle attachment, add the butter and beat on medium speed until smooth, about 1 minute. Add the granulated and brown sugars and continue beating on medium-high speed until fluffy and lighter in color, 2 to 3 minutes.

**4.** Add 5 of the eggs, one at a time, beating until blended after each addition. Add the vanilla along with the remaining egg. Add one-third of the flour mixture and mix on low speed until just blended, about 30 seconds. Add half the milk and mix until just blended, about 30 seconds. Add another third of the flour mixture and mix on low speed until just blended, about 30 seconds. Add the remaining milk and mix until just blended, about 30 seconds. Add the remaining flour mixture and mix until just blended, about 30 seconds.

**5.** Drop small amounts of the batter, spacing them close together, over the apple slices and, using an offset spatula, spread evenly. Bake until a toothpick inserted in the center comes out clean, 34 to 36 minutes.

**SERVE THE CAKE**

**6.** Immediately run a paring knife around the inside rim of the pan. Set a large cutting board on top of the pan and invert the cake. Use caution, as the pan is heavy and very hot. Let the inverted pan rest for about 3 minutes to let the topping settle (some may leak out onto the board). Gently remove the pan and reposition any apples that stuck to the pan onto the cake.

**7.** Slice and serve or cover and store at room temperature for up to 4 days.

*flavor swaps*

**PEAR**   Use an equal amount of firm ripe pears in place of the apples.

**PEACH**   Use an equal amount of firm ripe peaches in place of the apples.

**THIS DECADENT CHEESECAKE** is an easier and faster-to-prepare version of one of America's favorite desserts. The crispy and salty pretzel crust offers a textural counterpoint to the smooth and creamy filling, while the caramel drizzle is the icing on this cake. A gorgeous make-ahead party dessert!

· · · · · · · · · · · · · · · · · · · · · · · · · · · · · · · · · · · · · · · · · · · · · · · · · · · · · · · · · · · · · ·

### crust

3 cups (11 oz/312 g) finely ground salted **pretzel crumbs**

⅓ cup (2⅜ oz/66 g) **granulated sugar**

¼ teaspoon **table salt**

2 sticks (1 cup/8 oz/227 g) **unsalted butter**, melted

### cake

6 packages (8 oz/227 g each) **cream cheese**, softened

2 tablespoons **cornstarch**

½ teaspoon **table salt**

2 cups (14 oz/397 g) **granulated sugar**

4 teaspoons **pure vanilla extract**

6 large **eggs**, at room temperature

### assembly and serving
**Caramel Sauce** (page 160)

### flavor swaps

**BERRY** In place of the Caramel Sauce, use the Double Berry Sauce (page 164).

**BUTTERSCOTCH** In place of the granulated sugar in the cake, use 1¾ cups (12¼ oz/350 g) packed dark brown sugar.

**DULCE DE LECHE** In place of the Caramel Sauce, use a can of store-bought dulce de leche.

serves
**12 to 16**

### BAKE THE CRUST

**1.** Position a rack in the center of the oven and preheat the oven to 350°F (180°C/gas mark 4). Have an ungreased half-sheet pan ready.

**2.** Combine the pretzel crumbs, sugar, and salt in a medium bowl and, using a fork, stir until blended. Add the melted butter and mix until the crumbs are evenly moist and clump together slightly. Scrape the mixture into the pan and, using a flat-bottom measuring cup, press evenly onto the bottom and up the sides of the pan. Bake until the crust is fragrant and slightly darkened, 9 to 11 minutes. Let the pan cool on a rack. Lower the oven temperature to 300°F (150°C/gas mark 2).

### BAKE THE CAKE

**3.** In the bowl of a stand mixer fitted with the paddle attachment, beat the cream cheese, cornstarch, and salt on medium speed, scraping down the sides of the bowl and the paddle frequently, until very smooth and fluffy, about 5 minutes. Add the sugar and continue beating until well blended and smooth, about 3 more minutes. Add the vanilla and beat until blended, about 30 seconds. Add the eggs, one at a time, beating on medium speed just until blended. Scrape the filling into the cooled crust and, using an offset spatula, spread evenly.

**4.** Bake until the center jiggles slightly when nudged, 34 to 36 minutes. The cake will be slightly puffed around the edges and the center will still look moist.

**5.** Let the cake cool in the pan.

**6.** Refrigerate for at least 1 hour, then cover loosely with plastic and continue to chill until set, 8 hours or up to 2 days, before serving.

### ASSEMBLE AND SERVE THE CAKE

**7.** About 1 hour before serving, remove the cake from the refrigerator. Drizzle some of the sauce over the top, if using.

# stacked cakes

*A stacked sheet cake has the same visual appeal as a classic* layer cake. Once baked, the sheet-pan cake layer is cooled, cut into three rounds or four rectangles, sandwiched with a variety of frostings or fillings, and, if desired, covered with more of the same. Finishing touches and accompaniments can be casual or more elevated, as time and interest permit.

All types of cakes can be stacked, so you'll see lots of sponges, soufflés, angel foods, and chiffons. They also come with a sweet bonus: once you cut and remove the layers from the pan, any leftover cake pieces can be transformed into soft or crisp buttery croutons to top your cake or can be turned into fine crumbs to cover all or some of a frosted cake. These croutons and crumbs are also delicious sprinkled over yogurt, ice cream, or fruit and can be mixed with frosting and formed into cake pops or truffles.

Each stacked cake follows a similar path for unmolding, preparation, and assembly. The following steps are referenced in each recipe. That said, there are a few exceptions that are described in the instructions, so be sure to read carefully.

## unmolding and preparing the cake

Remove the cake from the oven and place it on a rack. Using a gentle sawing motion, run the tip of a small knife around the edges to loosen the cake from the pan. Let cool for 15 minutes. Cover the pan with a rack large enough to extend beyond the edges of the pan. Using pot-holders, grip both racks, with the sheet pan sandwiched between, and flip to invert. Lift the top rack and the pan from the cake and carefully peel away the parchment. Cover the cake with the same rack and, again gripping both racks, flip to invert so the top side of the cake is up again. Let cool completely.

## assembling and serving the cake

Three-layer stacked cakes can be round or rectangular. To make a three-layer round cake, use an inverted plate or cardboard template and the tip of a small knife to cut out three 6¾-inch (16.7 centimeter) circles. To make a four-layer rectangular cake, use the tip of a small knife to cut the cake in half along the 18-inch (46 centimeter) length, then cut again in half along the 13-inch (33 centimeter) length to make four rectangles that are approximately 9 by 6½ inches (23 by 16.5 centimeters). Brush away any crumbs from the sides of the layers. Save any remaining cake scraps or use the extra rectangular layer to make croutons or cake crumbs (see page 18), if you like.

Put one cake layer, top side up, on a flat serving plate. (To protect the plate from smears during frosting, you may want to slip small strips of foil or parchment between the cake and the plate.) If the recipe calls for a soak, use a small pastry brush to brush the soak evenly over the first cake layer. Pile 1 to 1¼ cups of frosting onto the cake layer and spread evenly to the edges. Place the next layer, top side up, on top of the frosting. Align the sides and gently press down on the layer.

Brush the soak, if using, on the second layer, and spread another 1 to 1¼ cups of the frosting evenly to the cake's edge. Place the third layer, top side down, on top of the frosting. Align the sides and gently press down on that layer.

If you are frosting the outside of the cake, spread a thin layer of the remaining frosting over the sides and top of the cake to seal in any pesky crumbs (this is a crumb coat). Refrigerate the cake for 10 to 15 minutes. Spread as much of the remaining frosting as you like evenly over the sides and top of the cake.

Just before serving, pile the cake crumbs or croutons on top of the cake, if using. Or, using a cupped hand, gently press some of the cake crumbs around the sides and top of the cake to cover completely. Add any additional garnishes.

**THREE LAYERS OF FLUFFY, VANILLA-SCENTED CAKE** and an American-style buttercream made with high-quality white chocolate (I like Lindt) are already amazingly delicious, but I take things a step further by piling this cake high with a blizzard of cake crumbs. Far from cloying and overly rich, a slice of this cake is refreshingly light and thoroughly divine.

*serves*
**12 to 16**

### cake

4 large **eggs**, separated, at room temperature

1¾ cups (12¼ oz/350 g) **granulated sugar**

2½ cups (10 oz/283 g) **cake flour**

1 tablespoon **baking powder**

1 teaspoon **table salt**

¾ cup (6 oz/170 g) **whole milk**, at room temperature

1 stick (½ cup/4 oz/113 g) **unsalted butter**, melted and cooled

3 tablespoons **neutral oil**

1 tablespoon **pure vanilla extract**

### assembly and serving

**White Chocolate Frosting** (full recipe, page 149)

**Cake crumbs** (see page 18), soft or toasted (optional)

### BAKE THE CAKE

**1.** Position a rack in the center of the oven and preheat the oven to 350°F (180°C/gas mark 4). Lightly grease the bottom and sides of the half-sheet pan. Line the bottom with parchment and lightly grease and flour the bottom and sides.

**2.** In the bowl of a stand mixer fitted with the whisk attachment, beat the egg whites on medium-low speed until foamy, about 1 minute. Increase the speed to medium and beat until the whites form soft peaks, 1 to 2 minutes. Continue beating and slowly add ¼ cup (1¾ oz/50 g) of the sugar. Beat until the whites are thick, shiny, and form medium-firm peaks, 2 to 3 more minutes. Scrape the whites into a medium bowl and wipe out the mixer bowl.

**3.** Sift the flour into the mixer bowl and add the remaining 1½ cups (10½ oz/298 g) sugar, the egg yolks, the baking powder, salt, milk, butter, oil, and vanilla. Mix with the paddle attachment on low speed for about 15 seconds, then increase the speed to medium high and beat until the mixture is well blended, 1 to 2 more minutes.

**4.** Scrape one-fourth of the whites into the flour mixture and, using a rubber spatula, gently stir until blended. Add the remaining whites and gently fold until just blended with no visible streaks of the whites.

**5.** Scrape the batter into the prepared pan and, using an offset spatula, spread evenly. Bake until a toothpick inserted in the center comes out clean, 17 to 19 minutes.

**6.** Unmold the cake, let cool, and cut out 3 circles or 4 rectangles (see page 67).

## ASSEMBLE AND SERVE THE CAKE

**7.** Fill and assemble the cake layers, using half of the frosting (see page 67). Cover with the top layer. Spread the remaining frosting on the top and sides of the cake.

**8.** Follow the directions for storing and serving the cake (see page 21). Just before serving, scatter cake crumbs over the top of the cake, if desired.

### *flavor swaps*

**CHOCOLATE**   Use the Vanilla Buttercream Frosting (full recipe, Double Chocolate variation; pages 150 and 151) in place of the White Chocolate Frosting.

**PEACH**   Use the Vanilla Mascarpone Cream Frosting (full recipe, with Crushed Fruit add-in using peaches; pages 145 and 153) in place of the White Chocolate Frosting.

**THE BANANA-CHOCOLATE FLAVOR COMBO** continues to be a favorite at Dodge family birthday celebrations. Because it bakes up so quickly, this cake is perfect for weeknight dinners or parties.

*serves*
**12 to 16**

## cake

2⅔ cups (12 oz/340 g) **unbleached all-purpose flour**

1 tablespoon **baking powder**

½ teaspoon **table salt**

¼ teaspoon **baking soda**

2 sticks (1 cup/8 oz/227 g) **unsalted butter**, softened

1 cup (7 oz/198 g) **granulated sugar**

½ cup (3½ oz/99 g) packed **light brown sugar**

4 large **eggs**, at room temperature

2 teaspoons **pure vanilla extract**

3 very ripe medium **bananas**, mashed (about 1 cup/9 oz/255 g)

½ cup (4¼ oz/120 g) **buttermilk**, at room temperature

## assembly and serving

**Vanilla Buttercream Frosting** (full recipe, Double Chocolate variation; pages 150 and 151)

**Cake croutons** (see page 18), soft or toasted (optional)

**Banana slices** (optional)

### BAKE THE CAKE

**1.** Position a rack in the center of the oven and preheat the oven to 350°F (180°C/gas mark 4). Lightly grease the bottom and sides of the half-sheet pan. Line the bottom with parchment and lightly grease and flour the bottom and sides.

**2.** Combine the flour, baking powder, salt, and baking soda in a medium bowl and whisk until blended. In the bowl of a stand mixer fitted with the paddle attachment, beat the butter on medium speed until smooth, about 1 minute. Add the granulated and brown sugars and continue beating on medium-high speed until fluffy and lighter in color, 2 to 3 more minutes.

**3.** Add 3 of the eggs, one at a time, beating until blended after each addition. Add the vanilla along with the remaining egg. Add one-third of the flour mixture and mix on low speed until just blended, about 30 seconds. Add the mashed bananas and mix until just blended, about 30 seconds more. Add another third of the flour mixture and mix on low speed until just blended, about 30 seconds. Add the buttermilk and mix until just blended, about 30 seconds. Add the remaining flour mixture and mix until just blended, about 30 seconds.

**4.** Scrape the batter into the prepared pan and, using an offset spatula, spread evenly. Bake until a toothpick inserted in the center comes out clean, 20 to 22 minutes.

**5.** Unmold the cake, let cool, and cut out 3 circles or 4 rectangles (see page 67).

### ASSEMBLE AND SERVE THE CAKE

**6.** Fill and assemble the cake layers, using about half the buttercream on the bottom layers (see page 67). Top with the final layer. Spread the remaining frosting on the top and sides of the cake.

**7.** Follow the directions for storing and serving the cake (see page 21). Just before serving, scatter cake croutons and banana slices over the top of the cake, if desired.

*flavor swaps*

**MARSHMALLOW CHIP**    Use the Vanilla Marshmallow Frosting (full recipe, with Chocolate Chips add-in; pages 142 and 153) in place of the buttercream.

**TOFFEE-BANANA**    Use the Vanilla Cream Cheese Frosting (full recipe, Brown Sugar variation; page 139) in place of the buttercream. Just before serving, gently press handfuls of toffee pieces around the sides of the cake to cover completely.

**PICNIC DINNERS ON THE BEACH** are what my summers are all about. Cool salty breezes and clean high tides, along with the company of dear friends at the picnic table are some of my fondest memories. This cake was inspired by one such friend. Tim Herrmann (an epic baker) made the most delectable, gorgeous cake for his mom-in-law's birthday. As he and I discussed every element of his creation, I knew that this stacked version had to be included here for you to enjoy.

*cake*

5 tablespoons (2½ oz/ 71 g) **whole milk**

¼ cup (1⅞ oz/53 g) **olive oil** (light and fruity extra-virgin)

1½ teaspoons **pure vanilla extract**

1⅓ cups (5⅜ oz/152 g) **cake flour**

2 teaspoons **baking powder**

1 teaspoon **table salt**

8 large **eggs**, at room temperature

1⅓ cups (9⅜ oz/266 g) **granulated sugar**

½ cup (1½ oz/42 g) **unsweetened natural cocoa powder**, sifted

**BAKE THE CAKE**

**1.** Position a rack in the center of the oven and preheat the oven to 350°F (180°C/gas mark 4). Lightly grease the bottom and sides of the half-sheet pan. Line the bottom with parchment and lightly grease and flour the bottom and sides.

**2.** In a small saucepan, or in a heatproof container in the microwave for 15-second increments, heat the milk until very hot but not boiling. Stir in the olive oil and vanilla.

**3.** Combine the flour, baking powder, and salt in a medium bowl and whisk until blended. In the bowl of a stand mixer fitted with the whisk attachment, beat the eggs on medium-high speed until pale in color, about 3 minutes. Gradually add the sugar and continue beating until a ribbon of batter forms in the bowl when the beater is lifted, about 3 more minutes.

**4.** Add the cocoa and mix briefly on low speed until just barely blended, about 15 seconds. With the mixer running, gradually add the hot milk mixture and mix briefly until just blended, about 15 seconds. Sift the flour mixture into the bowl and fold in, using a rubber spatula, until completely combined.

**5.** Scrape the batter into the prepared pan and, using an offset spatula, spread evenly. Bake until a toothpick inserted in the center comes out clean, 15 to 17 minutes.

**6.** Unmold the cake, let cool, and cut it into 3 circles or 4 rectangles (see page 67).

*serves*
**12 *to* 16**

## assembly and serving

**Classic Soak** (Boozy variation using dark rum; page 156)

**Vanilla Mascarpone Cream Frosting** (half recipe, with Crushed Fruit add-in using fresh cherries; pages 145 and 153)

**Vanilla Buttercream Frosting** (half recipe, Double Chocolate variation; pages 150 and 151)

Pitted fresh **cherries**, for garnish (optional)

**Cake croutons** (see page 18), soft, for garnish (optional)

### ASSEMBLE AND SERVE THE CAKE

**7.** Assemble the cake, brushing the bottom layers with the soak and then spreading the mascarpone cream on the layers. Top with the final layer, then spread the buttercream frosting on the top and the sides of the cake (see page 67).

**8.** Follow the directions for storing and serving the cake (see page 21). Just before serving, scatter cherries and cake croutons over the top of the cake, if desired.

### flavor swap

**WHITE CHOCOLATE-STRAWBERRY**   Use the Vanilla Mascarpone Cream Frosting (half recipe, with Crushed Fruit add-in using strawberries; pages 145 and 153) in place of the cherry-flavored frosting. Use the White Chocolate Frosting (half recipe, page 149) in place of the chocolate-flavored buttercream. Garnish with halved fresh strawberries in place of the cherries.

ICE CREAM HOLDS A SPECIAL SPOT IN MY HEART, and this brownie–ice cream combo hits all the right notes. The flavor pairing is a tip of the hat to traditional cinnamon-spiked Mexican hot chocolate, topped with a pointed pile of marshmallow in place of the usual whipped cream. If you have a kitchen blowtorch, feel free to give the marshmallow spikes a campfire flavor. I like to cut the brownie remainders from the pan into bite-size pieces and store them in the freezer. Just like cake croutons, they make a great snack and are delicious stirred into oatmeal or bread puddings.

Note: To make quick work at go-time, cut the cake into serving pieces in advance and refreeze the portions on your serving plate. This way, the cake still looks amazing and the slices are ready to enjoy.

## brownie layers

1¾ cups (7⅞ oz/223 g) **unbleached all-purpose flour**

2 teaspoons **ground cinnamon**

1 teaspoon **baking powder**

½ teaspoon **table salt**

3 sticks (1½ cups/12 oz/340 g) **unsalted butter**

1½ cups (4½ oz/128 g) **unsweetened natural cocoa powder**, sifted

3 cups (21 oz/596 g) **granulated sugar**

4 large **eggs**

2 teaspoons **pure vanilla extract**

1 cup (4 oz/113 g) chopped **walnuts** (optional)

## assembly and serving

2 (1-pint) containers **chocolate ice cream**

**Vanilla Marshmallow Frosting** (half recipe, with Citrus add-in using orange zest; pages 142 and 153)

### BAKE THE BROWNIE LAYERS

**1.** Position a rack in the center of the oven and preheat the oven to 325°F (170°C/gas mark 3). Lightly grease the bottom and sides of the half-sheet pan. Line the bottom with parchment and lightly grease and flour the bottom and sides.

**2.** Combine the flour, cinnamon, baking powder, and salt in a medium bowl and whisk until well blended. Melt the butter in a medium saucepan and set over medium-low heat, stirring occasionally, about 2 minutes. Remove the pan from the heat and whisk in the cocoa powder until smooth. Add the sugar and whisk until blended. Using your fingertip, check the temperature of the batter, it should be warm but not hot. If it's hot, set the pan aside for a minute or so.

**3.** Add the eggs, 2 at a time, and the vanilla to the batter and whisk until well blended. Add the flour mixture and stir with a rubber spatula until just blended. Scrape the batter into the prepared pan and, using an offset spatula, spread evenly. If using, scatter the nuts over the top. Bake until a toothpick inserted in the center comes out with small bits of brownie sticking to it, 17 to 19 minutes.

**4.** Unmold the brownie, let cool, and cut out two 8-inch (20 cm) circles (see page 67).

### ASSEMBLE AND SERVE THE CAKE

**5.** Remove the bottom from an 8-inch (20 cm) round springform pan with 3-inch (7.5 cm) sides and place the ring on a flat serving plate. Make room

serves
**12 to 16**

*continued*

in your freezer for the cake. Place 1 brownie layer, top side up, in the center of the ring. Pile all the ice cream on top of the brownie layer. Place a piece of plastic wrap directly on the ice cream and use the palm of your hand or the bottom of a measuring cup to spread it into an even layer. Remove the plastic.

**6.** Place the remaining brownie layer, top side up, on the ice cream and press gently. Cover the pan with plastic wrap and freeze until set and very firm, at least 8 hours or up to 3 days.

**7.** Remove the cake from the freezer. Dip a thin knife into hot tap water, wipe dry, and run it around the inside of the ring to loosen the cake. Unclasp the springform ring and remove. Scrape the frosting onto the brownie layer and spread evenly to completely cover the top of the cake. Using a rubber spatula or the back of a spoon, pull the frosting up to create spiky points. Serve immediately or freeze for at least 1 hour before wrapping and freezing for up to 2 days.

**8.** Just before serving, cut into slices.

*flavor swap*

**PEPPERMINT** In place of the cinnamon in the cake, stir in ½ teaspoon pure peppermint oil or extract along with the eggs. In place of the chocolate ice cream, use mint chocolate chip ice cream. In place of the orange zest in the frosting, use ¼ teaspoon pure peppermint oil or extract.

**I LOVE ALL GIRL SCOUT COOKIES,** but I admit to being partial to their Thin Mints. Those crisp cookies make the most of two bold flavors. Unlike when you make the other stacked cakes, you'll use all four layers of this delicious soufflé cake. It is as delicious as the cookies and will impress your guests. When it's time to assemble the cake, it's best to work with very cold layers.

## cake

1 cup (6 oz/170 g) chopped **bittersweet chocolate**

½ cup (4 oz/113 g) **water**

6 tablespoons (1⅛ oz/ 32 g) **unsweetened natural cocoa powder**, sifted

5 tablespoons (2½ oz/71 g) **unsalted butter**, cut into pieces

1 cup (7 oz/198 g) **granulated sugar**

8 large **eggs**, separated, at room temperature

2 teaspoons **pure vanilla extract**

½ teaspoon **pure peppermint oil** or **extract**

¼ teaspoon **table salt**

## assembly and serving

**Bittersweet Chocolate Ganache** (half recipe, page 140)

**Vanilla Buttercream Frosting** (half recipe, page 150)

2 cups (8 oz/227 g) ground **Thin Mints**, or other **chocolate-peppermint cookie**

**Bittersweet Chocolate Glaze or Sauce** (page 157), warmed (optional)

**Mint sprigs**, for garnish

### BAKE THE CAKE

**1.** Position a rack in the center of the oven and preheat the oven to 350°F (180°C/gas mark 4). Lightly grease the bottom and sides of the half-sheet pan. Line the bottom with parchment and lightly grease and flour the bottom and sides.

**2.** Combine the chocolate, water, cocoa powder, and butter in a large, heatproof bowl. Set the bowl over a pan of simmering water and whisk until the chocolate and butter are melted and the mixture is smooth, 3 to 4 minutes. (Alternatively, you can do this in the microwave in a heatproof measuring cup or bowl in 30-second increments.) Carefully remove the bowl and set on the counter. Whisk in about half the sugar until blended, about 30 seconds. Add the egg yolks, vanilla, peppermint oil, and salt and whisk until the mixture is smooth and well blended, about 1 minute.

**3.** In the bowl of a stand mixer fitted with the whisk attachment, beat the egg whites on medium-low speed until foamy, 1 to 2 minutes. Increase the speed to medium and beat until the whites form soft peaks, 1 to 2 more minutes. Continue beating while slowly adding the remaining sugar. Beat until the whites are thick, shiny, and form medium-firm peaks, 2 to 3 more minutes.

**4.** Scrape about one-fourth of the whites into the chocolate mixture and, using a rubber spatula, gently stir until blended. Add the remaining whites and gently fold in until just blended with no visible streaks of the whites.

**5.** Scrape the batter into the prepared pan and, using an offset spatula, spread evenly. Bake until the top springs back when lightly touched, 15 to 18 minutes.

**6.** Unmold the layer, let cool, then refrigerate until very cold, 2 to 4 hours. Cut out four 4 by 12-inch (10 by 30.5 cm) rectangles.

*serves*
**12 to 16**

*continued*

## ASSEMBLE AND SERVE THE CAKE

**7.** Spread the bottom 3 layers (using a long offset spatula for easy lifting and positioning) with the ganache. Top with the final layer and press down gently. Spread the buttercream on the top and sides of the cake (see page 67).

**8.** Follow the directions for storing and serving the cake (see page 21). Just before serving, using a cupped hand, gently press the cookie crumbs around the sides of the cake to cover completely. Arrange the mint sprigs on top. Slice and serve with a drizzle of the glaze, if desired.

### *flavor swap*

**DOUBLE RASPBERRY**   Omit the peppermint oil or extract from the cake. Use the Vanilla Mascarpone Cream Frosting (full recipe, Fruit Puree variation using fresh raspberries; pages 145 and 146) instead of the ganache and buttercream combination. Spread half the frosting on the bottom 3 layers and divide 1 cup (5 oz/142 g) fresh raspberries among the layers. Top with the final layer and coat the top and sides of the cake with the remaining frosting. Top the cake with additional raspberries and mint sprigs. Omit the cookie crumbs from the garnish.

**IF YOUR IDEA OF A DESSERT** begins with a dreamy, vanilla-infused cream filling between rum-soaked cake layers and ends with a thick coating of bittersweet chocolate glaze, then stop your search right here and now.

serves
**12 to 16**

### cake

2½ cups (11¼ oz/319 g) **unbleached all-purpose flour**

1¾ teaspoons **baking powder**

¼ teaspoon **baking soda**

¾ teaspoon **table salt**

2 sticks (1 cup/8 oz/227 g) **unsalted butter**, softened

1¾ cups (12¼ oz/350 g) **granulated sugar**

4 large **eggs**, at room temperature

1 tablespoon **pure vanilla extract**

1¼ cups (10⅝ oz/301 g) **buttermilk**, at room temperature

### assembly and serving

**Vanilla Pastry Cream** (half recipe; page 143)

**Classic Soak** (Boozy variation using dark rum; page 156)

**Bittersweet Chocolate Glaze or Sauce** (page 157), warmed

**Cake crumbs** (see page 18), soft (optional)

### flavor swap

**ESPRESSO** ⋅ Use the Classic Soak (Coffee variation; page 156) in place of the Boozy variation. Use the Vanilla Mascarpone Cream Frosting (half recipe, Mocha variation; page 145) in place of the pastry cream.

### BAKE THE CAKE

**1.** Position a rack in the center of the oven and preheat the oven to 350°F (180°C/gas mark 4). Lightly grease the bottom and sides of the half-sheet pan. Line the bottom with parchment and lightly grease and flour the bottom and sides.

**2.** Combine the flour, baking powder, baking soda, and salt in a medium bowl and whisk until blended. In the bowl of a stand mixer fitted with the paddle attachment, beat the butter on medium speed until smooth, about 1 minute. Add the sugar and continue beating on medium-high speed until fluffy and lighter in color, 2 to 3 more minutes.

**3.** Add 3 of the eggs, one at a time, beating until blended after each addition. Add the vanilla along with the remaining egg. Add one-third of the flour mixture and mix on low speed until just blended, about 30 seconds. Add half the buttermilk and mix until just blended, about 30 seconds. Repeat with the second third of the flour and remaining butter-milk, ending with the final third of the flour mixture.

**4.** Scrape the batter into the prepared pan and, using an offset spatula, spread evenly. Bake until a toothpick inserted in the center comes out clean, 18 to 20 minutes.

**5.** Unmold the cake, let cool, and cut out 3 circles or 4 rectangles (see page 67).

### ASSEMBLE AND SERVE THE CAKE

**6.** Reserve about 1 cup of the pastry cream.

**7.** Fill and assemble the cake layers using an even amount of the soak on the bottom layers. Spread the remaining pastry cream on the bottom layers. Top with the final layer and spread the reserved pastry cream on the sides of the cake. Spread the glaze evenly over the top, just to the edge.

**8.** Follow the directions for storing and serving the cake (see page 21). Just before serving, scatter cake crumbs over the side edges of the cake, if desired.

**USE YOUR SHEET PAN TO WHIP UP** a light-as-a-feather angel food cake in a fraction of the time it takes to make the classic. The stacked cake is delicious topped with a double hit of apricot (both jam and fruit), chopped crystallized ginger, and luscious whipped cream. A drizzle of caramel sauce on top is nice, if you have the time.

## cake

1 cup (4 oz/113 g) **cake flour**

1 cup (4 oz/113 g) **confectioners' sugar**

2½ teaspoons **ground ginger**

½ teaspoon **table salt**

10 large **egg whites**, at room temperature

1 teaspoon **cream of tartar**

¾ cup (5¼ oz/149 g) **granulated sugar**

1½ teaspoons **pure vanilla extract**

## assembly and serving

½ cup (6 oz/170 g) **apricot jam**

**Vanilla Mascarpone Cream Frosting** (half recipe, with Crushed Fruit add-in using apricots; pages 145 and 153)

Fresh **apricot** wedges

Chopped **crystallized ginger**

**Cake croutons** (see page 18), soft or toasted

## flavor swap

**LEMON CURD** · Use ½ cup of the Lemon Curd (page 159) in place of the jam. Use the Whipped Lemon Curd Cream (page 148) in place of the apricot-flavored mascarpone cream.

### BAKE THE CAKE

**1.** Position a rack in the center of the oven and preheat the oven to 350°F (180°C/gas mark 4). Lightly grease the bottom and sides of the half-sheet pan. Line the bottom with parchment and lightly grease and flour the bottom and sides.

**2.** Sift together the cake flour, confectioners' sugar, ginger, and salt 3 times onto a sheet of parchment.

**3.** In the bowl of a stand mixer fitted with the whisk attachment, beat the egg whites and cream of tartar on medium-low speed until foamy, about 1 minute. Increase the speed to medium, and beat until the whites form soft peaks, 1 to 2 minutes. Continue beating while slowly adding the granulated sugar. Beat until the whites are thick, shiny, and form medium-firm peaks, 2 to 3 more minutes. Add the vanilla and mix briefly until blended.

**4.** Sift about one-fourth of the flour mixture over the beaten whites and gently fold in, using a rubber spatula, until just blended. Repeat with the remaining flour mixture, one-fourth at a time.

**5.** Scrape the batter into the prepared pan and, using an offset spatula, spread evenly. Bake until the top springs back when lightly touched, 16 to 18 minutes.

**6.** Unmold the cake, let cool, and cut out 3 circles or 4 rectangles (see page 67).

### ASSEMBLE AND SERVE THE CAKE

**7.** Assemble the cake, spreading the bottom layers with the jam, then spreading about two-thirds of the frosting on the layers. Top with the final layer, then spread the remaining frosting on the top of the cake (see page 67).

**8.** Follow the directions for storing and serving the cake (see page 21). Just before serving, top the cake with apricots, crystallized ginger, and croutons. Slice and serve with additional apricot wedges, if desired.

*serves*
**12 to 16**

**MY BROTHER TIM HAS A DEEP-ROOTED LOVE OF GINGERBREAD,** and so our mom always enjoyed treating him to his favorite dessert. As the dessert was "his," he was first to choose and he always chose the middle piece. My guess is that he didn't care for the crusty, chewy edges. With deep notes of molasses and spice, and without a single crusty edge, this stacked cake is a nod to my big brother.

*serves*
**12 to 16**

## cake

3 cups (13½ oz/383 g) **unbleached all-purpose flour**

4¼ teaspoons **ground ginger**

2¼ teaspoons **ground cinnamon**

1 teaspoon **baking soda**

½ teaspoon **table salt**

¼ teaspoon **ground nutmeg**

2 sticks (1 cup/8 oz/227 g) **unsalted butter**, softened

½ cup (3½ oz/99 g) packed **dark brown sugar**

½ cup (3½ oz/99 g) **granulated sugar**

2 large **eggs**, at room temperature

1 cup (8½ oz/241 g) **buttermilk**, at room temperature

1 cup (12 oz/340 g) light **molasses**

½ cup (2 oz/57 g) finely chopped **walnuts**, toasted (optional)

## assembly and serving

**Vanilla Cream Cheese Frosting** (full recipe, Cranberry Jam variation; page 139)

**Cake crumbs** (see page 18), soft

**Sugared Cranberries** (page 86)

### BAKE THE CAKE

**1.** Position a rack in the center of the oven and preheat the oven to 350°F (180°C/gas mark 4). Lightly grease the bottom and sides of the half-sheet pan. Line the bottom with parchment and lightly grease and flour the bottom and sides.

**2.** Combine the flour, ginger, cinnamon, baking soda, salt, and nutmeg in a medium bowl and whisk until blended. In the bowl of a stand mixer fitted with the paddle attachment, beat the butter on medium speed until smooth, about 1 minute. Add the brown and granulated sugars and continue beating on medium-high speed until fluffy and lighter in color, 2 to 3 more minutes.

**3.** Add the eggs, one at a time, beating until blended after each addition. Add one-third of the flour mixture and mix on low speed until just blended, about 30 seconds. Add the buttermilk and mix until just blended, about 30 seconds. Repeat with the second third of the flour and the molasses, ending with the final third of the flour mixture along with the walnuts, if using.

**4.** Scrape the batter into the prepared pan and, using an offset spatula, spread evenly. Bake until a toothpick inserted in the center comes out clean, 18 to 20 minutes.

**5.** Unmold the cake, let cool, and cut out 3 circles or 4 rectangles (see page 67).

### ASSEMBLE AND SERVE THE CAKE

**6.** Assemble the cake layers, spreading about half the frosting on the bottom layers. Top with the final layer and spread the remaining frosting on the top and sides of the cake (see page 67).

*continued*

**7.** Follow the directions for storing and serving the cake (see page 21). Just before serving, scatter cake crumbs over the top of the cake, if desired. Top with Sugared Cranberries.

### flavor swaps

**HONEY** Use the Vanilla Cream Cheese Frosting (full recipe, Honey variation; page 139) in place of the cranberry frosting. Serve with a drizzle of honey.

**MALTED MILK** Use the Vanilla Buttercream Frosting (full recipe, Malted Milk variation; pages 150 and 151) in place of the cream cheese frosting. Serve with a sprinkle or so of malted milk powder.

## SUGARED CRANBERRIES

*makes about 2 cups (about 6¹/₂ oz/184 g)*

Combine ½ cup (4 oz/113 g) tap water and ½ cup (3½ oz/99 g) granulated sugar in a small saucepan. Bring to a boil, stirring occasionally, over medium heat. Add 1½ cups (5¼ oz/149 g) fresh cranberries, reduce heat to low and simmer, stirring occasionally, about 1 minute. Slide the pan from the heat, set aside, and cool to room temperature.

Arrange a cooling rack over a sheet pan. Using a slotted spoon, move the cranberries to the rack and let dry until slightly tacky, 20 to 30 minutes. The syrup can be strained, covered, and stored in the refrigerator for up to 5 days. It's delicious stirred into seltzer or used as a cocktail fixing.

Put ⅔ cup (2⅜ oz/66 g) granulated sugar in a shallow bowl, add some of the cranberries, and, using a spoon or your fingertips, roll the cranberries to coat completely. Return the coated berries to the rack to dry completely. Repeat with the remaining berries and sugar. Cover and store at room temperature up to 2 days.

*sheet cake*

**THE APPLE BUTTER LENDS A SPECTACULAR TENDERNESS** to this cake's texture, and the subtle but distinct, slightly sweet apple flavor comes through with only a hint of cinnamon spice. In lieu of a more traditional filling, there's an apple brandy soak and more unsweetened apple butter. The cake is then covered with a brown sugar cream cheese frosting. This cake is elegant and sophisticated, a real departure from traditional apple cakes.

## cake

7 large **eggs**, separated, at room temperature

1¼ cups (8¾ oz/248 g) packed **light brown sugar**

2⅓ cups (10½ oz/298 g) **unbleached all-purpose flour**

2½ teaspoons **baking powder**

1¾ teaspoons **ground cinnamon**

1¼ teaspoons **table salt**

1¼ cups (10½ oz/198 g) unsweetened **apple butter**, at room temperature

¾ cup (5⅞ oz/167 g) **neutral oil**

2½ teaspoons **pure vanilla extract**

## assembly and serving

**Classic Soak** (Boozy variation using apple brandy; page 156)

1 cup (8½ oz/241 g) **apple butter**, lightly sweetened or unsweetened

**Vanilla Cream Cheese Frosting** (half recipe, Brown Sugar variation; page 139)

**Apple Compote** (recipe follows)

## BAKE THE CAKE

**1.** Position a rack in the center of the oven and heat the oven to 350°F (180°C/gas mark 4). Lightly grease the bottom and sides of the half-sheet pan. Line the bottom with parchment and lightly grease and flour the bottom and sides.

**2.** In the bowl of a stand mixer fitted with the whisk attachment, beat the egg whites on medium-low speed until foamy, about 1 minute. Increase the speed to medium and beat until the whites form soft peaks, 1 to 2 minutes. Continue beating while slowly adding ½ cup (3½ ounces/99 grams) of the brown sugar. Beat until the whites are thick, shiny, and form medium-firm peaks, 2 to 4 minutes. Scrape the whites into a medium bowl and wipe out the mixer bowl.

**3.** Sift the flour into the mixer bowl, add the remaining ¾ cup (5¼ ounces/149 grams) brown sugar, the egg yolks, the baking powder, cinnamon, salt, apple butter, oil, and vanilla and mix with the paddle attachment on medium-low speed until blended, about 15 seconds. Increase the speed to medium high and beat until the mixture is well blended, 1 to 2 minutes.

**4.** Scrape about one-fourth of the whites into the flour mixture and, using a rubber spatula, gently stir until blended. Add the remaining whites and gently fold in until just blended with no visible streaks of the whites.

**5.** Scrape the batter into the prepared pan and, using an offset spatula, spread evenly. Bake until a toothpick inserted in the center comes out clean, 12 to 14 minutes.

**6.** Unmold, let cool, and cut 3 rounds or 4 rectangles (see page 67).

*serves*
**12 *to* 16**

*continued*

**ASSEMBLE AND SERVE THE CAKE**

**7.** Assemble the cake layers, brushing the bottom layers with the soak and spreading with the apple butter. Top with the final layer, then spread the frosting evenly on the top and sides of the cake (see page 67).

**8.** Follow the directions for storing and serving the cake (see page 21). Slice and serve with some of the compote.

*flavor swap*

**PEAR**    Use pear butter in place of the apple butter in the cake and filling. Flavor the soak with pear brandy instead of the apple brandy. Use pears or a combination of apples and pears in the compote.

## APPLE COMPOTE

*makes about 1 1/2 cups (7 1/2 oz/213 g)*

2 tablespoons (1 oz/28 g) **unsalted butter**

3 cups (15 oz/425 g) coarsely chopped **apples**, such as Granny Smith or Golden Delicious

2 tablespoons **granulated sugar**

In a medium skillet, melt the butter over medium-low heat. Add the apples and cook, stirring frequently, until golden brown around the edges, 5 to 7 minutes. Reduce the heat to low, add the sugar, and cook, stirring frequently, until the apples are very tender when pierced with the tip of a knife, 4 to 6 minutes. Serve warm or at room temperature. Leftovers can be stored in the refrigerator for up to 4 days.

**I BELIEVE NOTHING SAYS "HAPPY"** quite like a cake with rainbow-colored sprinkles. This light and airy cake filled with smooth vanilla buttercream that is spiked with crushed strawberries is guaranteed to be the star of every party—birthday or not—so make sure it has a place of honor at the table.

## cake

2½ cups (11¼ oz/319 g) **unbleached all-purpose flour**

1¾ teaspoons **baking powder**

¼ teaspoon **baking soda**

¾ teaspoon **table salt**

2 sticks (1 cup/8 oz/227 g) **unsalted butter**, softened

1¾ cups (12¼ oz/350 g) **granulated sugar**

3 large **eggs**, at room temperature

1 large **egg yolk**, at room temperature

1 tablespoon **pure vanilla extract**

1¼ cups (10 oz/283 g) **whole milk**, at room temperature

⅓ cup (2 oz/57 g) **multicolored sprinkles**

## assembly and serving

**Classic Soak** (page 156; optional)

**Vanilla Buttercream Frosting** (full recipe, with Crushed Fruit add-in using strawberries; pages 150 and 153)

**Cake croutons** (see page 18), soft or toasted

**Multicolored sprinkles** (optional)

### BAKE THE CAKE

**1.** Position a rack in the center of the oven and preheat the oven to 350°F (180°C/gas mark 4). Lightly grease the bottom and sides of the half-sheet pan. Line the bottom with parchment and lightly grease and flour the bottom and sides.

**2.** Combine the flour, baking powder, baking soda, and salt in a medium bowl and whisk until blended. In the bowl of a stand mixer fitted with the paddle attachment, beat the butter on medium speed until smooth, about 1 minute. Add the sugar and continue beating on medium-high speed until fluffy and lighter in color, 2 to 3 more minutes.

**3.** Add 2 of the eggs and the yolk, one at a time, beating until blended after each addition. Add the vanilla along with the remaining egg. Add one-third of the flour mixture and mix on low speed until just blended, about 30 seconds. Add half the milk and mix until just blended, about 30 seconds. Repeat with the second third of the flour and the remaining milk, ending with the final third of the flour mixture. Fold in the sprinkles until just blended.

**4.** Scrape the batter into the prepared pan and, using an offset spatula, spread evenly. Bake until a toothpick inserted in the center comes out clean, 20 to 22 minutes.

**5.** Unmold the cake, let cool, and cut out 3 rounds or 4 rectangles (see page 67).

### ASSEMBLE AND SERVE THE CAKE

**6.** Assemble the cake, brushing the bottom layers with the soak, if using, then using about half the frosting for the filling. Top with the final layer. Spread the remaining frosting on the top and sides of the cake (see page 67).

**7.** Follow the directions for storing and serving the cake (see page 21). Just before serving, scatter croutons and sprinkles on top of the cake, if desired.

*serves*
**12 to 16**

**I HAVE A FAIR SHARE OF IRISH IN ME** and I'm darn proud of it. This cake is scrappy, fun, friendly (just like my family), and deliciously addictive. No, you don't have to serve this only on St. Paddy's. No, you don't have to add the food coloring. But for some fun-filled Irish celebrating, add its Kelly green glory!

serves
**12 to 16**

## cake

2⅓ cups (10½ oz/298 g) **unbleached all-purpose flour**

1⅓ cups (9⅜ oz/266 g) **granulated sugar**

¼ cup (¾ oz/20 g) **unsweetened natural cocoa powder**, sifted

¾ teaspoon **table salt**

1¼ cups (9⅝ oz/273 g) **neutral oil**

1 cup (8½ oz/241 g) **buttermilk**, at room temperature

2 large **eggs**, at room temperature

2 teaspoons **pure vanilla extract**

1 teaspoon **white vinegar**

1 teaspoon **baking soda**

½ teaspoon **green food coloring gel**, or 2 teaspoons liquid food coloring (optional)

## assembly and serving

**Classic Soak** (Boozy variation using Bailey's Irish Cream; page 156)

**Vanilla Buttercream Frosting** (full recipe, Boozy variation using Bailey's Irish Cream; pages 150 and 151)

**Bittersweet Chocolate Glaze or Sauce** (page 157), warmed (optional)

### BAKE THE CAKE

**1.** Position a rack in the center of the oven and preheat the oven to 350°F (180°C/gas mark 4). Lightly grease the bottom and sides of the half-sheet pan. Line the bottom with parchment and lightly grease and flour the bottom and sides.

**2.** Combine the flour, sugar, cocoa powder, and salt in the bowl of a stand mixer fitted with the paddle attachment and mix on medium-low speed until blended, about 30 seconds. Add the oil, buttermilk, and eggs and beat on medium speed until just blended, about 1 minute. Stir the vanilla, vinegar, baking soda, and food coloring, if using, in a ramekin and add to the mixer bowl. Mix on medium-low speed until just blended, about 30 seconds.

**3.** Scrape the batter into the prepared pan and, using an offset spatula, spread evenly. Bake until a toothpick inserted in the center comes out clean, 16 to 18 minutes.

**4.** Unmold the cake, let cool completely, and cut out 3 rounds or 4 rectangles (see page 67).

### ASSEMBLE AND SERVE THE CAKE

**5.** Assemble the cake, brushing the bottom layers with the soak, if using. Use about half the frosting for the filling. Top with the final layer. Spread the remaining frosting on the top and sides of the cake (see page 67).

**6.** Follow the directions for storing and serving the cake (see page 21). Slice and serve with a drizzle of the glaze, if desired.

### flavor swap

**CREAM CHEESE**   Use the Vanilla Cream Cheese Frosting (full recipe, Brown Sugar variation; page 139) in place of the Bailey's-flavored buttercream.

I DIDN'T TRULY APPRECIATE HAZELNUTS until I was living in Paris during my culinary training. Each little nut packs rich, earthy flavor and pairs beautifully with a wide variety of fillings and frostings.

## cake

1½ cups (6¾ oz/191 g) **unbleached all-purpose flour**

⅔ cup (2⅝ oz/74 g) finely ground toasted **hazelnuts**

1½ teaspoons **baking powder**

¾ teaspoon **table salt**

6 large **eggs**, at room temperature

1 cup (7 oz/198 g) packed **light brown sugar**

2 tablespoons **neutral oil**

2 teaspoons **pure vanilla extract**, or 2 tablespoons hazelnut liqueur

## assembly and serving

**Classic Soak** (Boozy variation using hazelnut liquor; page 156; optional)

**Vanilla Mascarpone Cream Frosting** (half recipe, Nutella variation; page 145)

**Vanilla Buttercream Frosting** (half recipe, Nut variation using hazelnuts; pages 150 and 152)

**Cake croutons** (see page 18)

A handful of toasted **hazelnuts**, coarsely chopped

### BAKE THE CAKE

**1.** Position a rack in the center of the oven and preheat the oven to 350°F (180°C/gas mark 4). Lightly grease the bottom and sides of the half-sheet pan. Line the bottom with parchment and lightly grease and flour the bottom and sides.

**2.** Combine the flour, ground nuts, baking powder, and salt in a medium bowl and whisk until blended. In the bowl of a stand mixer fitted with the whisk attachment, beat the eggs on medium-high speed until pale in color, about 2 minutes. Gradually add the brown sugar and continue beating until the mixture has tripled in volume and a ribbon of batter falls from the beater when lifted, about 2 minutes. Combine the oil and vanilla and beat on medium speed until blended, about 1 minute. Sprinkle half the flour mixture over the egg mixture and gently fold, using a rubber spatula, until just blended. Repeat with the remaining flour.

**3.** Scrape the batter into the prepared pan and, using an offset spatula, spread evenly. Bake until a toothpick inserted in the center comes out clean, 13 to 15 minutes.

**4.** Unmold the cake, let cool, and cut out 3 rounds or 4 rectangles (see page 67).

### ASSEMBLE AND SERVE THE CAKE

**5.** Assemble the cake layers, brushing the bottom layers with the soak, if using, then adding the mascarpone cream between the layers. Top with the final layer. Spread the buttercream frosting evenly over the top and sides of the cake.

**6.** Follow the directions for storing and serving the cake (see page 21). Just before serving, scatter cake croutons and hazelnuts over the top of the cake.

### flavor swap

**HONEY CREAM CHEESE** Use the Vanilla Cream Cheese Frosting (full recipe, Honey variation; page 139) in place of the mascarpone and buttercream.

*serves*
**12 to 16**

**AS SOON AS THE SUMMER BERRY SEASON BEGINS,** I start dreaming about this cake. The tender layers are lemon scented, paired with a veritable explosion of raspberries and mounds of berry cream filling.

## cake

½ cup (4 oz/113 g) **whole milk**

5 tablespoons (2½ oz/71 g) **unsalted butter**, cut into pieces

1¾ cups (7⅞ oz/223 g) **unbleached all-purpose flour**

1 tablespoon **baking powder**

1 teaspoon **table salt**

7 large **eggs**, at room temperature

1½ cups (10½ oz/298 g) **granulated sugar**

2 teaspoons finely grated **lemon zest**

½ teaspoon pure **lemon extract** or oil

## assembly and serving

½ cup (5½ oz/156 g) **raspberry jam**

1 cup (5 oz/142 g) fresh **raspberries**, rinsed and dried, plus more for garnish

**Vanilla Mascarpone Cream Frosting** (half recipe, Fruit Puree variation using raspberries; pages 145 and 146)

**Cake croutons** (see page 18)

*serves*
**12 to 16**

### BAKE THE CAKE

**1.** Position a rack in the center of the oven and preheat the oven to 350°F (180°C/gas mark 4). Lightly grease the bottom and sides of the half-sheet pan. Line the bottom with parchment and lightly grease and flour the bottom and sides.

**2.** In a small saucepan over medium-low heat, or in a heatproof container in the microwave for 15-second increments, heat the milk and butter together until the butter is melted and the mixture is very hot but not boiling.

**3.** Combine the flour, baking powder, and salt in a medium bowl and whisk until blended. In the bowl of a stand mixer fitted with the whisk attachment, beat the eggs on medium-high speed until pale and foamy, about 3 minutes. Gradually add the sugar, lemon zest, and extract and continue beating until a ribbon of batter falls from the beater when lifted, about 3 more minutes.

**4.** With the mixer on medium-low speed, gradually add the flour mixture and mix until just blended, about 15 seconds. With the mixer still on medium-low speed, gradually add the hot milk mixture and mix until just blended, about 15 seconds.

**5.** Scrape the batter into the prepared pan and, using an offset spatula, spread evenly. Bake until a toothpick inserted in the center comes out clean, 14 to 16 minutes.

**6.** Unmold the cake, let cool, and cut out 3 rounds or 4 rectangles (see page 67).

### ASSEMBLE AND SERVE THE CAKE

**7.** Fill and assemble the stacked cake using the jam on the bottom two layers. Sprinkle half the berries on those layers, then use one-third of the mascarpone as filling between the layers. Top with the remaining layer, and spread the top of the cake with the remaining mascarpone (see page 67).

**8.** Follow the directions for storing and serving the cake (see page 21). Just before serving, scatter cake croutons and raspberries over the top of the cake.

## flavor swaps

**LEMON** • Use the Vanilla Buttercream Frosting (half recipe, with Citrus add-in using lemon zest; pages 150 and 153) in place of the raspberry-flavored mascarpone cream.

**BLUEBERRY** • Use an equal amount of blueberry jam in place of the raspberry jam and fresh blueberries instead of raspberries for the fruit filling. Use blueberries instead of raspberries as the Fruit Puree variation of the mascarpone cream.

**THE FLAVORS IN THIS CAKE ARE REMINISCENT** of that coffeehouse favorite, a flat white, which is a smaller latte with less frothy steamed milk, hence a higher proportion of coffee to milk. The smooth, velvety buttercream pairs nicely with the espresso- and coffee-infused cake layers to mimic the hot brew. The result is a melt-in-your-mouth cake that is a coffee lover's dream.

*serves*
**12 to 16**

### cake

6 large **eggs**, separated, at room temperature

1¾ cups (12¼ oz/350 g) packed **light brown sugar**

2 cups (9 oz/255 g) **all-purpose flour**

2 teaspoons **baking powder**

1 teaspoon **table salt**

1 cup (8½ oz/241 g) **sour cream**, at room temperature

⅔ cup (5⅛ oz/145 g) **neutral oil**

5 teaspoons **instant espresso powder**

1 tablespoon **pure vanilla extract**

### assembly and serving

½ cup (2 oz/57 g) toasted **walnuts**, finely chopped

**Vanilla Buttercream Frosting** (full recipe, page 150)

**Classic Soak** (Coffee variation; page 156)

**Cake croutons** (see page 18)

### BAKE THE CAKE

**1.** Position a rack in the center of the oven and heat the oven to 350°F (180°C/gas mark 4). Lightly grease the bottom and sides of the half-sheet pan. Line the bottom with parchment and lightly grease and flour the bottom and sides.

**2.** In the bowl of a stand mixer fitted with the whisk attachment, beat the egg whites on medium-low speed until foamy, about 1 minute. Increase the speed to medium and beat until the whites form very soft peaks, 1 to 2 minutes. Continue beating while slowly adding ½ cup (3½ oz/99 g) of the brown sugar. Beat until the whites are thick, shiny, and form medium-firm peaks, 2 to 3 more minutes. Scrape the whites into a medium bowl and wipe out the inside of the mixer bowl.

**3.** Add the flour to the mixer bowl, then add the remaining 1¼ cups (8¾ oz/248 g) brown sugar, the baking powder, salt, egg yolks, sour cream, oil, espresso powder, and vanilla. Mix with the paddle attachment on medium-low speed for about 15 seconds, then increase the speed to medium high and beat until well blended, 1 to 2 minutes.

**4.** Scrape about one-fourth of the whites into the flour mixture and, using a rubber spatula, gently stir until blended. Add the remaining whites and gently fold in until just blended with no visible streaks of the whites.

**5.** Scrape the batter into the prepared pan and, using an offset spatula, spread evenly. Bake until a toothpick inserted in the center comes out clean, 16 to 18 minutes.

**6.** Unmold, let cool, and cut into 3 rounds or 4 rectangles (see page 67).

### ASSEMBLE AND SERVE THE CAKE

**7.** Add the toasted walnuts to half of the buttercream and stir until blended.

**8.** Assemble the cake, brushing the bottom layers with the soak and using the walnut-studded buttercream as the filling for those layers. Top with the final layer. Spread the remaining buttercream evenly on the top and sides of the cake (see page 67).

**9.** Follow the directions for storing and serving the cake (see page 21). Just before serving, scatter cake croutons over the top of the cake.

*flavor swaps*

**CHOCOLATE COOKIES AND CREAM**   When preparing the full recipe for Vanilla Buttercream Frosting, measure out half to mix with the Cookie Crumbs add-in using chocolate cookies (pages 150 and 153), and use that for the filling. Use the remaining buttercream to frost the top and sides of the cake.

**MOCHA**   Use the Vanilla Mascarpone Cream Frosting (full recipe, page 145) in place of the buttercream. Flavor half the mascarpone cream with the Mocha variation (page 145) and use that for the filling. Use the remaining mascarpone cream for frosting the top and sides of the cake.

**DEVOURING A GOOEY MIX OF SLIGHTLY CHARRED MARSHMALLOWS** and a slab of milk chocolate sandwiched between graham crackers is a summertime camp snack or backyard barbecue or fire pit favorite that few can resist. This is a riff on these ingredients and builds into a sumptuous and festive cake that is officially approved for year-round enjoyment.

......................................................................................

### cake

½ cup (4 oz/113 g) **whole milk**

5 tablespoons (2½ oz/71 g) **unsalted butter**, cut into pieces

2 teaspoons **pure vanilla extract**

1¾ cups (7⅞ oz/223 g) **unbleached all-purpose flour**

1 tablespoon **baking powder**

1 teaspoon **table salt**

7 large **eggs**, at room temperature

1¾ cups (12¼ oz/350 g) **granulated sugar**

⅔ cup (2⅝ oz/74 g) ground **graham crackers** (plain or cinnamon flavored)

### assembly and serving

**Bittersweet Chocolate Ganache** (half recipe, Milk Chocolate variation; page 140)

**Vanilla Marshmallow Frosting** (half recipe, with Cookie Crumbs add-in using graham crackers; pages 142 and 153)

2 cups (8 oz/227 g) **graham cracker crumbs**

**Chocolate Curls** (using milk chocolate; page 163; optional)

### BAKE THE CAKE

**1.** Position a rack in the center of the oven and heat the oven to 350°F (180°C/gas mark 4). Lightly grease the bottom and sides of the half-sheet pan. Line the bottom with parchment and lightly grease and flour the bottom and sides.

**2.** In a small saucepan over medium-low heat, or in a heatproof container in the microwave for 15-second increments, heat the milk and butter together until the butter is melted and the mixture is very hot but not boiling. Stir in the vanilla.

**3.** Combine the flour, baking powder, and salt in a medium bowl and whisk until blended. In the bowl of a stand mixer fitted with the whisk attachment (or use a handheld electric mixer), beat the eggs on medium-high speed until pale in color and foamy, about 3 minutes. Gradually add the sugar and continue beating until a ribbon of batter falls when the beater is lifted, about 3 minutes more.

**4.** With the mixer on medium-low speed, gradually add the flour mixture and mix until just blended, about 15 seconds. With the mixer on low speed, gradually add the hot milk mixture and mix briefly until just blended, about 15 seconds. Add the ground crackers and, using a rubber spatula, fold in until blended.

**5.** Scrape the batter into the prepared pan and, using an offset spatula, spread evenly. Bake until a toothpick inserted in the center comes out clean, 15 to 17 minutes.

**6.** Unmold, let cool, and cut out 3 rounds or 4 rectangles (see page 67).

### ASSEMBLE AND SERVE THE CAKE

**7.** Assemble the cake, spreading the ganache between the layers. Top with the final layer. Spread the frosting on the top and sides of the cake (see page 67). Coat the sides with the ground crackers and top with the chocolate curls, if desired.

serves
**12 to 16**

**8.** Follow the directions for storing and serving the cake (see page 21). Slice and serve.

*flavor swap*

**CHOCOLATE COOKIE CAKE**   Use an equal amount of chocolate graham crackers in place of the cinnamon or plain in the cake batter. Prepare a full recipe of Vanilla Buttercream Frosting (Double Chocolate variation, pages 150 and 151) in place of the ganache filling and marshmallow frosting.

# rolled cakes

*You'll likely be familiar with this version of a sheet cake.*
Think old-school jelly roll or a holiday Bûche de Noël, or yule log cake
(you'll find recipes for both here). Rolled cakes are baked in the half-
sheet pan, unmolded, and rolled up while still hot—that's when the
cake is most malleable. Sponge, hot milk, and chiffon cakes are the
most successful here, thanks to their more flexible structure.

Each rolled cake involves a similar method of unmolding,
preparing, and assembling. The following steps are referenced in each
recipe, so mark this page! That said, a few exceptions are noted in the
instructions, so do read carefully.

### unmolding and preparing the cake

Transfer the pan from the oven to a large cooling rack. Using a sawing motion, run the tip of a knife around the edges to loosen the cake
from the pan. Generously sift 1 cup (4 ounces/112 grams) confectioners' sugar over the cake. Cover the top of the cake completely with
two long strips of paper towels (or a clean tea towel), then place a
rack larger than the pan on top. Gripping both racks with oven mitts
(the pan is still hot), and with the sheet pan sandwiched in between,
flip the pan and racks to invert the cake. Lift the pan from the cake
and carefully peel away the parchment.

While the cake is still hot, beginning on one short side (or, to serve
16, one long side), roll up the cake and paper towel (or tea towel) layer
together. Place the cake seam side down (the cake edge will not be
directly under the cake but just to the side, facing down) on the rack
and let cool for 20 minutes to "train" the cake. Then, carefully unroll
the still-warm cake. It might look a bit wavy and uneven, and it might
have a few cracks; one end will be curled.

If the paper towel sticks to the cake and buckles a bit when unrolling, gently tear (or cut with a scissor) the paper towel to free the cake. Reposition the paper towel and continue unrolling. Sticking or buckling can happen if your environment is humid or if the cake is slightly underbaked. Next time, try baking your cake 1 minute longer.

## assembling and serving the cake

If the recipe calls for a soak, use a small pastry brush to spread the liquid evenly over the cake.

Scrape the filling onto the cake and spread it evenly to within ½ inch (12 millimeters) of one of the short sides and the two long edges, and to 1 inch (2.5 centimeters) of the remaining short side. Beginning with the short side (or, to serve 16, the long side), with the filling almost to the edge, gently roll the cake back up into a log. Using a long offset spatula, place the cake seam side down (the cake edge will not be directly under the cake but just to the side, facing down) on a flat serving plate or board.

If the recipe calls for a frosting or glaze, follow the instructions for when and how to add it.

The cake can be presented with its rustic edges or, if you prefer, cut away a bit to expose a cleaner look on the ends.

Rolled cakes can be cut into traditional ¾- to 1-inch-thick (2 to 2.5 centimeter) slices, or cut on alternate angles into wedges, 1½ to 2 inches (4 to 5 centimeters) thick at the wider end.

**HERE'S THE CLASSIC JELLY ROLL,** only slightly reimagined. It has the same tender crumb, same vanilla flavor, but is slightly less sweet and with a splash of poppy seeds for crunch. (Not into the poppy seeds? Just omit them.)

## cake

¼ cup (2 oz/57 g) **whole milk**

3 tablespoons (1½ oz/42 g) **unsalted butter**, cut into pieces

1½ teaspoons **pure vanilla extract**

1 cup plus 2 tablespoons (5 oz/142 g) **unbleached all-purpose flour**

1½ teaspoons **poppy seeds** (optional)

1¼ teaspoons **baking powder**

½ teaspoon **table salt**

4 large **eggs**, at room temperature

1 cup (7 oz/198 g) **granulated sugar**

## assembly and serving

1 cup (12 oz/340 g) **raspberry jam**, preferably seedless

**Confectioners' sugar**

**Lightly Sweetened Whipped Cream** (recipe follows; optional)

Handful of fresh **raspberries** (optional)

### BAKE THE CAKE

**1.** Position a rack in the center of the oven and preheat the oven to 350°F (180°C/gas mark 4). Lightly grease the bottom and sides of the half-sheet pan. Line the bottom with parchment and lightly grease and flour the bottom and sides.

**2.** In a small saucepan over medium-low heat, or in a heatproof container in the microwave for 15-second increments, heat the milk and butter together until the butter is melted and the mixture is very hot but not boiling. Stir in the vanilla.

**3.** Combine the flour, poppy seeds if using, baking powder, and salt in a medium bowl and whisk until blended. In the bowl of a stand mixer fitted with the whisk attachment, beat the eggs on medium-high speed until pale and foamy, about 3 minutes. Gradually add the sugar and continue beating until a ribbon of batter falls from the beater when lifted, about 3 minutes more.

**4.** With the mixer on medium-low speed, gradually add the flour mixture and mix until just blended, about 15 seconds. With the mixer on low speed, gradually add the hot milk mixture and mix again until just blended, about 15 seconds more.

**5.** Scrape the batter into the prepared pan and, using an offset spatula, spread evenly. Bake until the top of the cake springs back when lightly touched, 10 to 12 minutes.

**6.** Follow the directions for unmolding and preparing a rolled cake (see page 102).

*serves*
**12 to 16**

*continued*

**ASSEMBLE AND SERVE THE CAKE**

**7.** Spread the jam on the cake in an even layer, then reroll the cake and move to a serving plate (see page 103).

**8.** Follow the directions for storing and serving the cake (see page 21). Just before serving, dust the cake with the confectioners' sugar. Slice and serve with a dollop of whipped cream and a few raspberries, if desired.

*flavor swap*

**BERRY CHOICE**    Use an equal amount of any other flavor of jam or fruit butter in place of the raspberry.

## LIGHTLY SWEETENED WHIPPED CREAM

*makes 1¹/₂ cups*

¾ cup (6⅜ oz/181 g) **heavy cream**, chilled

2 tablespoons **granulated sugar**

½ teaspoon **pure vanilla extract**

Pour the heavy cream, sugar, and vanilla into a medium bowl. Beat with an electric handheld mixer fitted with wire beaters on medium speed until medium-firm peaks form when the beater is lifted. Use immediately or cover and refrigerate for up to 2 hours.

**THIS CAKE CAPTURES THE BUTTERY VANILLA** smell and smooth, creamy textures of a homemade stovetop butterscotch pudding, but in cake form. It's like eating a bowl of pudding with a lovely, soft cookie in each bite.

## cake

1 cup (4½ oz/128 g) **unbleached all-purpose flour**

1 teaspoon **baking powder**

½ teaspoon **table salt**

4 large **eggs**, at room temperature

1 large **egg white**, at room temperature

⅔ cup (4⅝ oz/131 g) packed **dark brown sugar**

1 tablespoon **neutral oil**

1½ teaspoons **pure vanilla extract**

## assembly and serving

**Vanilla Pastry Cream** (Butterscotch variation; page 143)

½ cup (2⅞ oz/82 g) **toffee bits**, plus more as desired

**Classic Soak** (Boozy variation using scotch whiskey; page 156)

### flavor swap

**VANILLA PUDDING**
Use dark rum to flavor the soak in place of the scotch. Use the Lightened Pastry Cream (page 143) in place of the Vanilla Pastry Cream. Top with the Bittersweet Chocolate Glaze or Sauce (White Chocolate variation; page 157) and scatter colored sprinkles on top instead of the toffee bits.

### BAKE THE CAKE

**1.** Position a rack in the center of the oven and preheat the oven to 350°F (180°C/gas mark 4). Lightly grease the bottom and sides of the half-sheet pan. Line the bottom with parchment and lightly grease and flour the bottom and sides.

**2.** Combine the flour, baking powder, and salt in a medium bowl and whisk until blended. In the bowl of a stand mixer fitted with the whisk attachment, beat the eggs and egg white on medium-high speed until pale in color, about 3 minutes. Gradually add the brown sugar and continue beating until a ribbon of batter falls from the beater when lifted, about 3 minutes. Add the oil and vanilla and beat on medium speed until blended, about 15 seconds more. Sift half the flour mixture over the eggs and, using a rubber spatula, fold in just until blended, about 1 minute. Repeat with the remaining flour.

**3.** Scrape the batter into the prepared pan and, using an offset spatula, spread evenly. Bake until the top springs back when lightly touched, 10 to 12 minutes.

**4.** Follow the directions for unmolding and preparing a rolled cake (see page 102).

### ASSEMBLE AND SERVE THE CAKE

**5.** Reserve about ¾ cup of the pastry cream, cover, and refrigerate until ready to serve. Fold the measured toffee pieces into the remaining pastry cream.

**6.** Unroll the cake and brush with the soak, then spread on the toffee pastry cream. Reroll the cake and move to a serving plate or board (see page 103).

**7.** Follow the directions for storing and serving the cake (see page 21). Just before serving, spread or pipe the reserved pastry cream evenly down the center of the cake and top with some additional toffee bits, if desired.

serves
**12 to 16**

EVER WONDER WHAT YOU WOULD END UP WITH if you marry a chocolate cake layer with a chocolate filling and cover it with a double chocolate buttercream? Some might say "a Bûche de Noël!" and others might say "a triple chocolate threat!" but the answer is both! During the holiday season, you can add some swirl markings to the buttercream and toss a few meringue mushrooms and chocolate curls onto the top and, poof, it's a Bûche. Other times, you can skip those elements and have yourself a divine and decadent chocolate dessert.

*serves*
**12 to 16**

### cake

3 tablespoons **whole milk**

2 tablespoons **neutral oil**

1 tablespoon **chocolate liqueur**, or 1½ teaspoons **pure vanilla extract**

1 teaspoon **instant espresso powder**

¾ cup (3 oz/85 g) **cake flour**

1 teaspoon **baking powder**

½ teaspoon **table salt**

5 large **eggs**, at room temperature

¾ cup (5¼ oz/149 g) packed **light brown sugar**

⅓ cup (1 oz/28 g) **unsweetened cocoa powder**

### assembly and serving

**Classic Soak** (Cream, Chocolate, or Coffee variation; page 156)

**Vanilla Mascarpone Cream Frosting** (half recipe, Mocha variation; page 145)

**Vanilla Buttercream Frosting** (half recipe, Double Chocolate variation; pages 150 and 151)

**Bittersweet Chocolate Glaze or Sauce** (page 157), warmed (optional)

### BAKE THE CAKE

**1.** Position a rack in the center of the oven and preheat the oven to 350°F (180°C/gas mark 4). Lightly grease the bottom and sides of the half-sheet pan. Line the bottom with parchment and lightly grease and flour the bottom and sides.

**2.** In a small saucepan over medium-low heat, or in a heatproof container in the microwave for 15-second increments, heat the milk until very hot but not boiling. Stir in the oil, liqueur, and espresso powder.

**3.** Combine the flour, baking powder, and salt in a medium bowl and whisk until blended. In the bowl of a stand mixer fitted with the whisk attachment, beat the eggs on medium-high speed until pale and foamy, about 3 minutes. Gradually add the brown sugar and continue beating until a ribbon of batter forms in the bowl when the beater is lifted, about 3 minutes more.

**4.** Add the cocoa and mix on low until just barely blended, about 15 seconds. With the mixer running, gradually add the hot milk mixture and mix on low until just blended, about 15 seconds more. Sift the flour mixture into the bowl and, using a rubber spatula, fold in until completely combined.

**5.** Scrape the batter into the prepared pan and, using an offset spatula, spread evenly. Bake until the top springs back when lightly touched, 9 to 11 minutes.

**6.** Follow the directions for unmolding and preparing a rolled cake (see page 102).

### ASSEMBLE AND SERVE THE CAKE

**7.** Unroll the cake and brush with the soak. Spread with the mascarpone cream, then reroll and move to a serving plate (see page 103). Spread the buttercream evenly over the cake.

**8.** Follow the directions for storing and serving the cake (see page 21). Just before serving, drizzle the cake with some of the warm glaze, if desired.

*flavor swap*

**BOOZY ORANGE**   Use the Cream Soak (page 156), not the Coffee or Chocolate variations. Use the Vanilla Buttercream Frosting (half recipe, Boozy variation using orange liqueur; pages 150 and 151) in place of the mascarpone cream. Use the White Chocolate Frosting (half recipe, page 149) in place of the chocolate-flavored buttercream. Garnish with finely grated orange zest and orange supremes (see Note on page 52), if desired.

**THIS ROLLED CAKE HAS ALL THE FLAVORS AND TEXTURES** of the classic tiramisù–a coffee-flavored Italian dessert–rolled into an elegant, easy-to-serve cake. This version of the Italian dessert is made with a vanilla sponge cake that is filled and frosted with a coffee-flavored whipped mascarpone cream and topped with shaved chocolate. What's even better is that it can, and should, be made ahead of time.

## cake

1½ teaspoons **pure vanilla extract**

¾ teaspoon **instant espresso powder**

1 cup (4½ oz/128 g) **unbleached all-purpose flour**

1 teaspoon **baking powder**

½ teaspoon **table salt**

4 large **eggs**, at room temperature

1 large **egg white**, at room temperature

⅔ cup (4⅝ oz/131 g) packed **light brown sugar**

## assembly and serving

⅓ cup (1½ oz/42 g) **Chocolate Shavings** (recipe follows)

**Vanilla Mascarpone Cream Frosting** (full recipe, Tiramisù variation; pages 145 and 146)

**Classic Soak** (Coffee variation; page 156)

**Chocolate Curls** (using dark chocolate; page 163)

**Confectioners' sugar** (optional)

### BAKE THE CAKE

**1.** Position a rack in the center of the oven and preheat the oven to 350°F (180°C/gas mark 4). Lightly grease the bottom and sides of the half-sheet pan. Line the bottom with parchment and lightly grease and flour the bottom and sides.

**2.** Combine the vanilla and espresso powder in a small bowl and stir to dissolve. Combine the flour, baking powder, and salt in a medium bowl and whisk until blended. In the bowl of a stand mixer fitted with the whisk attachment, beat the eggs and egg white on medium-high speed until pale in color, about 3 minutes. Gradually add the brown sugar and continue beating until a ribbon of batter falls from the beater when lifted, about 3 minutes. Add the espresso mixture and beat on medium speed until blended, about 15 seconds. Sift half the flour mixture over the eggs and gently fold in, using a rubber spatula, until just blended. Repeat with the remaining flour.

**3.** Scrape the batter into the prepared pan and, using an offset spatula, spread evenly. Bake until the top springs back when lightly touched, 11 to 13 minutes.

**4.** Follow the directions for unmolding and preparing a rolled cake (see page 102).

### ASSEMBLE AND SERVE THE CAKE

**5.** Fold the chocolate shavings into the frosting.

**6.** Unroll the cake and brush it with the soak, then spread on half the mascarpone cream. Reroll and transfer to a serving plate (see page 103). Spoon or pipe the remaining mascarpone cream evenly over the cake.

*continued*

*serves*
**12 *to* 16**

**7.** Follow the directions for storing and serving the cake (see page 21). Just before serving, top with the chocolate curls and a dusting of confectioners' sugar, if desired.

*flavor swap*

**LEMON ROLL** Use the Whipped Lemon Curd Cream (page 148) in place of the tiramisù flavor and use the Classic Soak (Citrus variation using lemon juice; page 156) in place of the coffee flavor. Use grated white chocolate and white chocolate curls instead of the dark chocolate.

## CHOCOLATE SHAVINGS

Chocolate shavings add a touch of texture and flavor to fillings and frostings. Line a half-sheet pan with parchment and set a box grater on top. Firmly slide the edge of a chocolate block over the large holes of the grater, letting the shavings fall onto the parchment. Fold the parchment around the chocolate shavings to fashion a chute and pour into a container or zip-top bag. Cover and store in the refrigerator for up to 6 months.

**DO YOU ENJOY A SALTY-SWEET DESSERT?** If so, you are in luck, because the flavor combo in this cake really hits the spot. Ground pretzels baked into the batter give the cake a salty flavor, which contrasts with the whipped caramel cream. A topping of more pretzels adds crunch and a drizzle of caramel sauce yields a spectacular dessert to share with your friends and family.

## cake

¼ cup (2 oz/57 g) **whole milk**

2 tablespoons (1 oz/28 g) **unsalted butter**, cut into pieces

1 tablespoon **neutral oil**

1½ teaspoons **pure vanilla extract**

1¼ cups (5⅝ oz/159 g) **unbleached all-purpose flour**

1½ teaspoons **baking powder**

½ teaspoon **table salt**

4 large **eggs**, at room temperature

⅓ cup (2⅜ oz/67 g) packed **light brown sugar**

½ cup (3½ oz/99 g) **granulated sugar**

½ cup (2 oz/57 g) finely ground **pretzels** (preferably lightly salted)

## assembly and serving

**Whipped Caramel Cream** (half recipe, page 147)

**Caramel Sauce** (page 160), warmed (optional)

Handful of small, thin **pretzels**

**Coarse sea salt** (optional)

*serves*
**12** *to* **16**

### BAKE THE CAKE

**1.** Position a rack in the center of the oven and preheat the oven to 350°F (180°C/gas mark 4). Lightly grease the bottom and sides of the half-sheet pan. Line the bottom with parchment and lightly grease and flour the bottom and sides.

**2.** In a small saucepan over medium-low heat, or in a heatproof container in the microwave for 15-second increments, heat the milk and butter together until the butter is melted and the mixture is very hot but not boiling. Stir in the oil and vanilla.

**3.** Combine the flour, baking powder, and salt in a medium bowl and whisk until blended. In the bowl of a stand mixer fitted with the whisk attachment, beat the eggs on medium-high speed until pale in color, about 3 minutes. Gradually add the brown and granulated sugars and continue beating until a ribbon of batter falls when the beater is lifted, about 3 more minutes.

**4.** With the mixer on medium-low speed, gradually add the flour mixture and mix just until blended, about 15 seconds. With the mixer on low speed, gradually add the hot milk mixture and mix briefly just until blended, about 15 seconds. Add the ground pretzels and fold in, using a rubber spatula, until blended.

**5.** Scrape the batter into the prepared pan and, using an offset spatula, spread evenly. Bake until the top of the cake springs back when lightly touched, 11 to 13 minutes.

**6.** Follow the directions for unmolding and preparing a rolled cake (see page 102).

**ASSEMBLE AND SERVE THE CAKE**

**7.** Reserve about ¾ cup of the caramel cream, cover, and refrigerate until serving.

**8.** Unroll and spread the cake with the remaining caramel cream, then reroll and move to a serving plate (see page 103).

**9.** Follow the directions for storing and serving the cake (see page 21). Just before serving, spread or pipe the reserved caramel cream evenly down the center of the cake. Drizzle some caramel sauce over the cake, arrange some pretzels in the cream, and sprinkle some sea salt over the top, if desired. Slice and serve with some of the warmed caramel sauce, if desired.

*flavor swap*

**CINNAMON CARAMEL** Use the Vanilla Buttercream Frosting (half recipe, with Cookie Crumbs add-in using cinnamon graham crackers; pages 150 and 153) in place of the caramel cream.

**MATCHA IS 100 PERCENT FINELY GROUND GREEN TEA LEAVES,** and it is known for its emerald green color. In its liquid form, matcha is a central component of traditional Japanese tea ceremonies, but the powder can also be added to cakes and many other baked goods, giving them an intriguing color, as well as taste. Good-quality matcha will have a slightly sweet flavor, with subtle vegetal or plantlike notes. Avoid lower-quality matcha, as the color and taste will not have the same effect.

## cake

¼ cup (2 oz/57 g) **whole milk**

3 tablespoons (1½ oz/42 g) **unsalted butter**, cut into pieces

1½ teaspoons **pure vanilla extract**

1 cup plus 2 tablespoons (5 oz/142 g) **unbleached all-purpose flour**

2 tablespoons **matcha**

1¼ teaspoons **baking powder**

½ teaspoon **table salt**

4 large **eggs**, at room temperature

1 cup (7 oz/198 g) **granulated sugar**

## assembly and serving

**Classic Soak** (Cream or Citrus variation using orange juice; page 156; optional)

**Vanilla Mascarpone Cream Frosting** (half recipe, Fruit Puree variation using strawberries; pages 145 and 146)

**Confectioners' sugar**

**Matcha powder**

**Lightly Sweetened Whipped Cream** (page 106; optional)

Handful of fresh **strawberries**, halved (optional)

### BAKE THE CAKE

**1.** Position a rack in the center of the oven and preheat the oven to 350°F (180°C/gas mark 4). Lightly grease the bottom and sides of the half-sheet pan. Line the bottom with parchment and lightly grease and flour the bottom and sides.

**2.** In a small saucepan over medium-low heat, or in a heatproof container in the microwave for 15-second increments, heat the milk and butter together until the butter is melted and the mixture is very hot but not boiling. Stir in the vanilla.

**3.** Combine the flour, matcha, baking powder, and salt in a medium bowl and whisk until blended. In the bowl of a stand mixer fitted with the whisk attachment, beat the eggs on medium-high speed until pale and foamy, about 3 minutes. Gradually add the sugar and continue beating until a ribbon of batter falls when the beater is lifted, about 3 minutes more.

**4.** With the mixer on medium-low speed, gradually add the flour mixture and mix just until blended, about 15 seconds. With the mixer on low speed, gradually add the hot milk mixture and mix briefly just until blended, about 15 seconds.

**5.** Scrape the batter into the prepared pan and, using an offset spatula, spread evenly. Bake until the top springs back when lightly touched, 11 to 13 minutes.

**6.** Follow the directions for unmolding and preparing a rolled cake (see page 102).

### ASSEMBLE AND SERVE THE CAKE

**7.** Unroll the cake, and first brush on the soak, if using, then spread on the mascarpone cream. Reroll and move to a serving plate (see page 103).

*continued*

*serves*
**12 to 16**

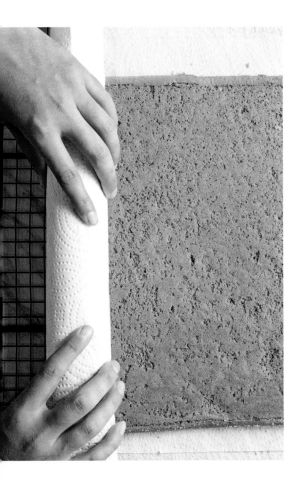

**8.** Follow the directions for storing and serving the cake (see page 21). Just before serving, dust the cake with some confectioners' sugar and top with a sprinkle of matcha powder. Slice and serve with a dollop of whipped cream and fresh strawberries, if desired.

*flavor swap*

**LEMON** ⚬ Choose the Classic Soak (Citrus variation using lemon juice; page 156). Use Vanilla Cream Cheese Frosting (half recipe, with Citrus add-in using lemon zest; pages 139 and 153) in place of the strawberry-flavored cream.

**THIS IS THE PERFECT HOLIDAY DESSERT** for anyone who's not a chocolate lover. It's fun and festive, and loaded with peppermint goodness. I'm all in favor of using real-deal candy canes as the garnish; just be sure to break them into bite-size pieces–they should be big enough to see their colorful stripes, but not so big that you'll need a visit to the dentist. For easy chopping, seal the medium canes in a heavy-duty zip-top bag, and break them using a rolling pin or a mallet. You want only the pieces, so sift out the fine powder–that's terrific stirred into hot chocolate or sprinkled over an ice cream sundae.

## cake

3 large **eggs**, separated, at room temperature

¾ cup (5¼ oz/149 g) **granulated sugar**

1 cup plus 2 tablespoons (4½ oz/128 g) **cake flour**

1¼ teaspoons **baking powder**

½ teaspoon **table salt**

¾ cup (5¾ oz/163 g) **neutral oil**

¼ cup (2⅛ oz/60 g) **sour cream**

1 teaspoon **pure vanilla extract**

¼ teaspoon **pure peppermint extract** or **oil**, plus more to taste

## assembly and serving

**White Chocolate Frosting** (half recipe, page 149)

**Classic Soak** (Peppermint variation; page 156)

Crushed **peppermint candy canes** or **hard candies** (optional)

### BAKE THE CAKE

**1.** Position a rack in the center of the oven and preheat the oven to 350°F (180°C/gas mark 4). Lightly grease the bottom and sides of the half-sheet pan. Line the bottom with parchment and lightly grease and flour the bottom and sides.

**2.** In the bowl of a stand mixer fitted with the whisk attachment, beat the egg whites on medium-low speed until foamy, about 1 minute. Increase the speed to medium and beat until the whites form soft peaks, 1 to 2 minutes. Continue beating and slowly add ¼ cup (1¾ oz/50 g) of the sugar. Beat until the whites are thick, shiny, and form medium-firm peaks, 2 to 3 minutes. Scrape the whites into a medium bowl and wipe out the mixer bowl.

**3.** Sift the flour into the mixer bowl and then add the remaining ½ cup (3½ oz/99 g) sugar, the egg yolks, the baking powder, salt, oil, sour cream, vanilla, and peppermint extract. Mix with the paddle attachment on medium-low speed for about 15 seconds, then increase the speed to medium high and beat until well blended, 1 to 2 minutes.

**4.** Scrape about one-fourth of the whites into the flour mixture and, using a rubber spatula, gently stir until blended. Add the remaining whites and gently fold in until just blended with no visible streaks of the whites.

**5.** Scrape the batter into the prepared pan and, using an offset spatula, spread evenly. Bake until the top springs back when lightly touched, 9 to 11 minutes.

**6.** Follow the directions for unmolding and preparing a rolled cake (see page 102).

*continued*

*serves*
**12 to 16**

**ASSEMBLE AND SERVE THE CAKE**

**7.** Reserve about ¾ cup of the frosting, cover, and refrigerate until serving.

**8.** Unroll the cake, then brush on the soak and spread with the remaining frosting. Reroll the cake and move to a serving plate (see page 103).

**9.** Follow the directions for storing and serving the cake (see page 21). Just before serving, spoon or pipe the reserved frosting down the center of the cake and scatter the peppermint candies over the top, if desired.

*flavor swap*

**SPRINKLES AND CREAM**   Use ½ teaspoon pure vanilla extract in place of the peppermint extract in the batter, and fold ¼ cup (1½ oz/42 g) of colored sprinkles into the cake batter. Use the Classic Soak (Cream variation; page 156) in place of the peppermint. Use the Vanilla Mascarpone Cream Frosting (half recipe, page 145) instead of the White Chocolate Frosting, and fold more sprinkles into the mascarpone cream. Garnish with additional sprinkles instead of the crushed peppermint.

**I LIKE TO DOUBLE (OR SHOULD I SAY TRIPLE?)** down on the maple flavorings for this lovely roll by pairing the maple-scented cake with a maple soak and a maple-flavored mascarpone cream. It's perfect for an evening's dessert, yet it's light enough for a lunch or teatime treat.

## cake

3 large **eggs**, separated, at room temperature

1 large **egg white**, at room temperature

¾ cup (5¼ oz/149 g) packed **dark brown sugar**

1 cup plus 2 tablespoons (4½ oz/128 g) **cake flour**

1 teaspoon **baking powder**

¼ teaspoon **table salt**

7 tablespoons (3⅜ oz/96 g) **neutral oil**

6 tablespoons (4⅛ oz/ 117 g) **pure maple syrup**

1 teaspoon **pure vanilla extract**

## assembly and serving

**Vanilla Mascarpone Cream Frosting** (half recipe, Maple variation; pages 145 and 146)

**Classic Soak** (Boozy variation using maple liqueur; page 156)

2 tablespoons finely chopped **walnuts**, toasted (optional)

### BAKE THE CAKE

**1.** Position a rack in the center of the oven and preheat the oven to 350°F (180°C/gas mark 4). Lightly grease the bottom and sides of the half-sheet pan. Line the bottom with parchment and lightly grease and flour the bottom and sides.

**2.** In the bowl of a stand mixer fitted with the whisk attachment, beat the egg whites on medium-low speed until foamy, about 1 minute. Increase the speed to medium and beat until the whites form soft peaks, 1 to 2 minutes. Continue beating and slowly add ¼ cup (1¾ oz/50 g) of the sugar. Beat until the whites are thick, shiny, and form medium-firm peaks, 2 to 3 minutes more. Scrape the whites into a medium bowl and wipe out the mixer bowl.

**3.** Sift the flour into the mixer bowl, then add the remaining ½ cup (3½ oz/100 g) brown sugar, the egg yolks, the baking powder, salt, oil, maple syrup, and vanilla. Mix with the paddle attachment on medium low speed for about 15 seconds, then increase the speed to medium high and beat until the mixture is well blended, 1 to 2 minutes.

**4.** Scrape about one-fourth of the whites into the flour mixture and, using a rubber spatula, gently stir until blended. Add the remaining whites and gently fold in until just blended with no visible streaks of the whites.

**5.** Scrape the batter into the prepared pan and, using an offset spatula, spread evenly. Bake until the top springs back when lightly touched, 11 to 13 minutes.

**6.** Follow the directions for unmolding and preparing a rolled cake (see page 102).

## ASSEMBLE AND SERVE THE CAKE

**7.** Reserve about ¾ cup of the mascarpone cream, cover, and refrigerate until serving.

**8.** Unroll the cake and brush with the soak, then spread with the remaining mascarpone cream. Reroll and move to a serving plate (see page 103).

**9.** Follow the directions for serving and storing the cake (see page 21). Just before serving, spoon or pipe the reserved mascarpone cream down the center of the cake and scatter the walnuts on the top, if desired.

*flavor swap*

**WALNUT** Use the Vanilla Buttercream Frosting (half recipe, Nut variation using walnuts; pages 150 and 152) in place of the mascarpone cream.

**THIS TENDER CAKE HAS THE EXTRA SPECIAL ADVANTAGE** of being both chocolate *and* vanilla, and it pairs well with any flavor of ice cream or sorbet.

## cake

¼ cup (2 oz/57 g) **whole milk**

3 tablespoons (1½ oz/42 g) **unsalted butter**, cut into pieces

1½ teaspoons **pure vanilla extract**

1 cup plus 2 tablespoons (5 oz/142 g) **unbleached all-purpose flour**

1¼ teaspoons **baking powder**

½ teaspoon **table salt**

4 large **eggs**, at room temperature

1 cup (7 oz/198 g) **granulated sugar**

1 tablespoon **unsweetened natural cocoa powder**, sifted

## assembly and serving

⅓ cup (3⅝ oz/103 g) **raspberry jam**, stirred

4 cups (20 oz/567 g) **raspberry sorbet**, slightly softened

**Confectioners' sugar**

**Lightly Sweetened Whipped Cream** (page 106)

**Bittersweet Chocolate Glaze or Sauce** (page 157), warmed

Handful of fresh **raspberries** (optional)

### BAKE THE CAKE

**1.** Position a rack in the center of the oven and preheat the oven to 350°F (180°C/gas mark 4). Lightly grease the bottom and sides of the half-sheet pan. Line the bottom with parchment and lightly grease and flour the bottom and sides.

**2.** In a small saucepan over medium-low heat, or in a heatproof container in the microwave for 15-second increments, heat the milk and butter together until the butter is melted and the mixture is very hot but not boiling. Stir in the vanilla.

**3.** Combine the flour, baking powder, and salt in a medium bowl and whisk until blended. In the bowl of a stand mixer fitted with the whisk attachment, beat the eggs on medium-high speed until pale and foamy, about 3 minutes. Gradually add the sugar and continue beating until a ribbon of batter falls from the beater when lifted, about 3 minutes.

**4.** With the mixer on medium-low speed, gradually add the flour mixture and mix until just blended, about 15 seconds. With the mixer on low speed, gradually add the hot milk mixture and mix briefly until just blended, about 15 seconds.

**5.** Scrape 1½ cups (6⅓ oz/181 g) of the batter into a small bowl and, using a rubber spatula, fold in the cocoa powder. Scrape the remaining batter into the prepared pan and, using an offset spatula, spread evenly. Using a spoon, dollop the cocoa batter evenly over and use the tip of an offset spatula to gently swirl the batters together, being careful not to touch the bottom of the pan. Shake the pan gently to settle the batters. Bake until the top of the cake springs back when lightly touched, 10 to 12 minutes.

**6.** Follow the directions for unmolding and preparing a rolled cake (see page 102).

**ASSEMBLE AND SERVE THE CAKE**

**7.** Have ready a flat serving plate and arrange a level area in the freezer. Unroll the cake and spread the jam over the cake in an even layer.

**8.** Scrape the sorbet into a medium bowl and, using a large spoon, stir and chop until the sorbet is smooth but not melted (the texture should be similar to mashed potatoes). Working quickly, drop small scoopfuls of the sorbet evenly over the jam. Cover with plastic wrap and, using your fingers, gently spread the sorbet into an even layer just to the edges. Reroll the cake (see page 103).

**9.** Move the roll to the serving plate and cover with plastic wrap. Freeze until very firm, at least 8 hours or up to 3 days.

**10.** Follow the directions for storing and serving the cake (see page 21). Just before serving, dust the cake with sifted confectioners' sugar. Slice and serve with a dollop of whipped cream, a drizzle of the chocolate glaze, and a few raspberries, if desired.

*flavor swap*

**ORANGE**  Use orange marmalade in place of the raspberry jam, and use orange sorbet in place of the raspberry sorbet.

**THE HAPPY YELLOW COLORING OF THIS CAKE** will make it seem like a sunny, bright spring day any time of the year. The touch of finely ground cornmeal in the cake layer lends a lovely bite and texture; it also helps soak up all that lemon and cream filling.

. . . . . . . . . . . . . . . . . . . . . . . . . . . . . . . . . . . . . . . . . . . .

### cake

¼ cup (2 oz/58 g) **whole milk**

3 tablespoons (1½ oz/42 g) **unsalted butter**, cut into pieces

2 teaspoons finely grated **lemon zest**

1 teaspoon **pure vanilla extract**

1 cup (4½ oz/128 g) **unbleached all-purpose flour**

¼ cup (1⅛ oz/32 g) finely ground **yellow cornmeal**

1¼ teaspoons **baking powder**

½ teaspoon **table salt**

4 large **eggs**, at room temperature

1 cup (7 oz/198 g) **granulated sugar**

### assembly and serving

½ cup (4½ oz/128 g) **Lemon Curd** (page 159), plus (optional) more for serving

**Whipped Lemon Curd Cream** (half recipe; page 148)

**Confectioners' sugar**, for dusting (optional)

### flavor swap

**LEMON CREAM CHEESE**
Use the Vanilla Cream Cheese Frosting (half recipe, with Citrus add-in using lemon zest; pages 139 and 153) in place of the Lemon Curd and Whipped Lemon Curd Cream.

**BAKE THE CAKE**

**1.** Position a rack in the center of the oven and preheat the oven to 350°F (180°C/gas mark 4). Lightly grease the bottom and sides of the half-sheet pan. Line the bottom with parchment and lightly grease and flour the bottom and sides.

**2.** In a small saucepan over medium-low heat, or in a heatproof container in the microwave for 15-second increments, heat the milk and butter together until the butter is melted and the mixture is very hot but not boiling. Stir in the lemon zest and vanilla.

**3.** Combine the flour, cornmeal, baking powder, and salt in a medium bowl and whisk until blended. In the bowl of a stand mixer fitted with the whisk attachment, beat the eggs on medium-high speed until pale and foamy, about 3 minutes. Gradually add the sugar and continue beating until a ribbon of batter falls from the beater when lifted, about 3 minutes more.

**4.** With the mixer on medium-low speed, gradually add the flour mixture and mix until just blended, about 15 seconds. With the mixer on low speed, gradually add the hot milk mixture and mix again until just blended, about 15 seconds more.

**5.** Scrape the batter into the prepared pan and, using an offset spatula, spread evenly. Bake until the top of the cake springs back when lightly touched, 10 to 12 minutes.

**6.** Follow the directions for unmolding and preparing a rolled cake (see page 102).

**ASSEMBLE AND SERVE THE CAKE**

**7.** Unroll the cake, spreading the lemon curd evenly over the layer, then spread with the lemon curd cream. Reroll and move to a serving plate (see page 103).

**8.** Follow the directions for storing and serving the cake (see page 21). Just before serving, dust with confectioners' sugar, if desired. Slice and serve with extra lemon curd, if desired.

*serves*
**12 to 16**

**THIS IS A VARIATION ON THE FIRST ROLLED CAKE** I made with my mom. We baked together almost every Sunday afternoon, experimenting with all kinds of dessert recipes. This cake is sturdy for rolling, which makes it a great cake for beginners.

## cake

¾ cup (3⅜ oz/96 g) **unbleached all-purpose flour**

¾ teaspoon **baking powder**

½ teaspoon **table salt**

3 large **eggs**, at room temperature

1 large **egg white**, at room temperature

½ cup (3½ oz/99 g) **granulated sugar**

2 teaspoons finely grated **orange** or **lemon zest**

¾ teaspoon **pure vanilla extract**

½ teaspoon **pure orange** or **lemon extract**

## assembly and serving

**Vanilla Mascarpone Cream Frosting** (half recipe, with Crushed Fruit add-in using strawberries; pages 145 and 153)

**Classic Soak** (Citrus variation, using lemon or orange juice; page 156)

Handful of fresh **berries**

*serves*
**12 *to* 16**

### BAKE THE CAKE

**1.** Position a rack in the center of the oven and preheat the oven to 350°F (180°C/gas mark 4). Lightly grease the bottom and sides of the half-sheet pan. Line the bottom with parchment and lightly grease and flour the bottom and sides.

**2.** Combine the flour, baking powder, and salt in a medium bowl and whisk until blended. In the bowl of a stand mixer fitted with the whisk attachment, beat the eggs and the egg white on medium-high speed until pale in color, about 3 minutes. Gradually add the sugar and continue beating until a ribbon of batter falls from the beater when lifted, 3 more minutes. Add the zest, vanilla, and orange extract and beat briefly until blended, 15 seconds. Sift half the flour mixture over the eggs and, using a rubber spatula, gently fold in until just blended. Repeat with the remaining flour.

**3.** Scrape the batter into the prepared pan and, using an offset spatula, spread evenly. Bake until the top springs back when lightly touched, 9 to 11 minutes.

**4.** Follow the directions for unmolding and preparing a rolled cake (see page 102).

### ASSEMBLE AND SERVE THE CAKE

**5.** Reserve about ¾ cup of the mascarpone cream, cover, and refrigerate until serving.

**6.** Unroll the cake and brush with the soak. Spread with the remaining mascarpone cream and reroll (see page 103). Move the roll to a serving plate.

**7.** Follow the directions for storing and serving the cake (see page 21). Just before serving, spoon or pipe the reserved mascarpone down the center of the cake and top with a few fresh berries. Slice and serve with additional berries, if desired.

*flavor swaps*

**WHITE CHOCOLATE**
Use the White Chocolate
Frosting (half recipe,
page 149) in place of the
mascarpone cream.

**LEMON CREAM CHEESE**
Use the Vanilla Cream
Cheese Frosting (half
recipe, with Citrus add-in
using lemon zest; pages
139 and 153) in place of
the mascarpone cream.

THIS CAKE WAS BORN IN MY MOM'S BOX OF RECIPE CARDS; it was part of our Sunday afternoon baking sessions. Over the years, I've tweaked the technique and fine-tuned the ingredient proportions, but I still think of this as one of my mom's cakes. Originally, it was an untoasted walnut cake with just simple vanilla flavoring. I've switched to toasted pecans–for the best flavor, always toast your nuts–and I've added a touch of boozy heat.

serves
**12 to 16**

### cake

5 large **eggs**, separated, at room temperature

⅔ cup (4⅝ oz/131 g) packed **light brown sugar**

½ cup (1½ oz/42 g) **cake flour**

1½ cups (6 oz/170 g) coarsely chopped **pecans**, toasted and finely ground

1 teaspoon **baking powder**

1 teaspoon **ground cinnamon**

½ teaspoon **table salt**

½ stick (4 tablespoons/ 2 oz/57 g) **unsalted butter**, melted

2 tablespoons **neutral oil**

1 tablespoon **scotch whiskey** (or **water**)

1½ teaspoons **pure vanilla extract**

### assembly and serving

**Vanilla Buttercream Frosting** (half recipe, with Cookie Crumbs add-in using cinnamon graham crackers; pages 150 and 153)

**Bittersweet Chocolate Glaze or Sauce** (White Chocolate variation, page 157), cooled

2 tablespoons finely chopped toasted **pecans** (optional)

### BAKE THE CAKE

**1.** Position a rack in the center of the oven and preheat the oven to 350°F (180°C/gas mark 4). Lightly grease the bottom and sides of the half-sheet pan. Line the bottom with parchment and lightly grease and flour the bottom and sides.

**2.** In the bowl of a stand mixer fitted with the whisk attachment, beat the egg whites on medium-low speed until foamy, about 1 minute. Increase the speed to medium and beat until the whites form soft peaks, 1 to 2 minutes. Continue beating while slowly adding ⅓ cup (2⅜ oz/66 g) of the brown sugar. Beat until the whites are thick, shiny, and form medium-firm peaks, 2 to 3 more minutes. Scrape the whites into a medium bowl and wipe out the mixer bowl.

**3.** Sift the flour into the mixer bowl and add the nuts, the remaining ⅓ cup (2⅜ oz/66 g) brown sugar, the egg yolks, the baking powder, cinnamon, salt, melted butter, oil, scotch, and vanilla. Beat on medium-low speed until blended, about 15 seconds. Increase the speed to medium high and beat until the mixture is well blended, 1 to 2 more minutes.

**4.** Scrape one-fourth of the whites into the flour mixture and, using a rubber spatula, gently stir until blended. Add the remaining whites and gently fold in until just blended with no visible streaks of the whites.

**5.** Scrape the batter into the prepared pan and, using an offset spatula, spread evenly. Bake until the top springs back when lightly touched, 12 to 14 minutes.

**6.** Follow the directions for unmolding and preparing a rolled cake (see page 102).

**ASSEMBLE AND SERVE THE CAKE**

**7.** Unroll the cake and spread with the buttercream. Reroll and move to a serving plate (see page 103). Spread the glaze evenly over the cake so that it drips down the sides a bit.

**8.** Follow the directions for storing and serving the cake (see page 21). Just before serving, scatter the pecans on top, if desired.

*flavor swaps*

**NUTELLA**   Use the Vanilla Mascarpone Cream Frosting (half recipe, Nutella variation; page 145) in place of the cinnamon–graham cracker buttercream.

**ESPRESSO**   Use the Vanilla Buttercream Frosting (half recipe, Espresso variation; pages 150 and 151) in place of the cinnamon–graham cracker buttercream.

CHOCOLATE PEANUT BUTTER FANS, this one's for you. It's got it all: moist, chocolaty cake layered with a chocolate-studded peanut butter and cream cheese filling, topped with a thick coating of dark chocolate glaze.

........................................................................

## cake

3 tablespoons **whole milk**

2 tablespoons **neutral oil**

1 teaspoon **pure vanilla extract**

¾ cup (3 oz/85 g) **cake flour**

1 teaspoon **baking powder**

½ teaspoon **table salt**

5 large **eggs**, at room temperature

¾ cup (5¼ oz/149 g) **granulated sugar**

⅓ cup (1 oz/28 g) **unsweetened natural cocoa powder**

## assembly and serving

Classic Soak (page 156)

Vanilla Cream Cheese Frosting (half recipe, Peanut Butter variation, with Chocolate Chips add-in using bittersweet chocolate; pages 139 and 153)

Bittersweet Chocolate Glaze or Sauce (page 157), cooled

## flavor swap

**WHITE AND MILK CHOCOLATE** • Use the White Chocolate Frosting (half recipe, page 149) in place of the peanut-butter-flavored cream cheese frosting. Use the Milk Chocolate variation of the Bittersweet Chocolate Glaze or Sauce (page 157).

### BAKE THE CAKE

**1.** Position a rack in the center of the oven and preheat the oven to 350°F (180°C/gas mark 4). Lightly grease the bottom and sides of the half-sheet pan. Line the bottom with parchment and lightly grease and flour the bottom and sides.

**2.** In a small saucepan over medium-low heat, or in a heatproof container in the microwave for 15-second increments, heat the milk until very hot but not boiling. Stir in the oil and vanilla.

**3.** Combine the flour, baking powder, and salt in a medium bowl and whisk until blended. In the bowl of a stand mixer fitted with the paddle attachment, beat the eggs on medium-high speed until pale and foamy, about 3 minutes. Gradually add the sugar and continue beating until a ribbon of batter falls from the beater when lifted, about 3 more minutes.

**4.** Add the cocoa and mix briefly on low speed until just barely blended, about 15 seconds. With the mixer running, gradually add the hot milk mixture and mix briefly on low speed until just blended, about 15 seconds. Sift the flour mixture into the bowl and fold in, using a rubber spatula, until completely combined.

**5.** Scrape the batter into the prepared pan and, using an offset spatula, spread evenly. Bake until the top springs back when lightly touched, 9 to 11 minutes.

**6.** Follow the directions for unmolding and preparing a rolled cake (see page 102).

### ASSEMBLE AND SERVE THE CAKE

**7.** Unroll the cake and brush with the soak. Spread the frosting over the cake and reroll (see page 103). Move to a serving plate. Spread the glaze evenly over the cake roll so that it droops down the sides a bit.

**8.** Follow the directions for storing and serving the cake (see page 21).

*serves*
**12 to 16**

**MARSHMALLOW, CAKE, AND COOKIES.** Now, that's a combo that will make kids and kids-at-heart smile. I'm a lifelong Oreo fan, but if you have another chocolate cream-filled cookie that tops your list then, by all means, use it.

## cake

3 large **eggs**, separated, at room temperature

¾ cup (5¼ oz/149 g) **granulated sugar**

1 cup plus 2 tablespoons (4½ oz/128 g) **cake flour**

1½ teaspoons **baking powder**

½ teaspoon **table salt**

6 tablespoons (3⅛ oz/ 88 g) **buttermilk**, at room temperature

6 tablespoons (2⅞ oz/ 82 g) **neutral oil**

1½ teaspoons **pure vanilla extract**

¼ cup (1 oz/28 g) ground **chocolate cookies**, such as chocolate wafers

## assembly and serving

**Vanilla Marshmallow Frosting** (half recipe, page 142)

⅔ cup (2⅝ oz/74 g) coarsely chopped **Oreo cookies**, plus a handful (optional) for garnish

**Classic Soak** (Cream or Chocolate variation; page 156)

**Bittersweet Chocolate Glaze or Sauce** (page 157), warmed

**serves 12 to 16**

### BAKE THE CAKE

**1.** Position a rack in the center of the oven and preheat the oven to 350°F (180°C/gas mark 4). Lightly grease the bottom and sides of the half-sheet pan. Line the bottom with parchment and lightly grease and flour the bottom and sides.

**2.** In the bowl of a stand mixer fitted with the whisk attachment, beat the egg whites on medium-low speed until foamy, about 1 minute. Increase the speed to medium and beat until the whites form very soft peaks, 1 to 2 minutes. Continue beating while slowly adding ¼ cup (1¾ oz/50 g) of the sugar. Beat until the whites are thick, shiny, and form medium-firm peaks, 2 to 3 more minutes. Scrape the whites into a medium bowl and wipe out the inside of the mixer bowl.

**3.** Sift the flour into the mixer bowl, then add the remaining ½ cup (3½ oz/99 g) sugar, the egg yolks, the baking powder, salt, buttermilk, oil, and vanilla. Mix with the paddle attachment on medium-low speed for about 15 seconds, then increase the speed to medium high and beat until well blended, 1 to 2 minutes.

**4.** Scrape one-fourth of the whites into the flour mixture and, using a rubber spatula, gently stir until blended. Add the remaining whites and gently fold in until barely blended. Add the ground cookies and fold in until blended with no visible streaks of the whites.

**5.** Scrape the batter into the prepared pan and, using an offset spatula, spread evenly. Bake until the top springs back when lightly touched, 9 to 11 minutes.

**6.** Follow the directions for unmolding and preparing a rolled cake (page 102).

### ASSEMBLE AND SERVE THE CAKE

**7.** Reserve about ¾ cup of the frosting and fold the cookie pieces into the remainder.

**8.** Unroll and brush the cake with the soak, then spread with the plain frosting. Reroll the cake and move to a serving plate (see page 103). Spoon or pipe the reserved frosting with cookie crumbs down the center of the cake.

**9.** Follow the directions for storing and serving the cake (see page 21). Just before serving, scatter the cookie pieces on top, if desired. Slice and serve with the chocolate glaze.

*flavor swap*

**BITTERSWEET CHOCOLATE GANACHE**    Use the Bittersweet Chocolate Ganache (half recipe, page 140) in place of the marshmallow frosting.

# frostings and fillings

*These recipes make enough to fill and frost any of the cakes* in this book. Not all the cake styles need the same amount of filling and frosting, so I've presented ingredient quantities to make half recipes as well as full recipes. I've also included lots of flavor variations—called Flavor Swaps—and fun additions—called Add-Ins—to stir into some of the frostings. As I'm a big frosting fan, the yields are ample, but if you prefer less, you can dial them back and use any amount you prefer. There's no need to use all the frosting or filling, in fact. Besides, having leftovers stored in the fridge isn't a hardship—it can elevate a midnight snack to new heights. I promise.

*vanilla cream cheese frosting*

### full recipe

*makes about 5 cups (36 oz/1 kg)*

2 (8 oz/227 g) packages **cream cheese**, softened

3 cups (12 oz/340 g) **confectioners' sugar**, sifted

2 sticks (1 cup/8 oz/227 g) **unsalted butter**, softened

2 tablespoons **heavy cream**

4 teaspoons **pure vanilla extract** or **vanilla bean paste**

¼ teaspoon **table salt**, plus more as needed

### half recipe

*makes about 2¹⁄₂ cups (18 oz/511 g)*

1 (8 oz/227 g) package **cream cheese**, softened

1½ cups (6 oz/170 g) **confectioners' sugar**, sifted

1 stick (½ cup/4 oz/113 g) **unsalted butter**, softened

1 tablespoon **heavy cream**

2 teaspoons **pure vanilla extract** or **vanilla bean paste**

⅛ teaspoon **table salt**, plus more as needed

**1.** In the bowl of a stand mixer fitted with the paddle attachment, beat the cream cheese, confectioners' sugar, butter, cream, vanilla, and measured salt on medium-high speed until no lumps remain and the texture is light and fluffy, 3 to 4 minutes.

**2.** Store well covered or in heavy-duty zip-top bags with the air pushed out for up to 1 week in the refrigerator. Before using, bring to room temperature and beat until smooth and light.

*flavor swaps* *(see also frosting add-ins, page 153)*

### PEANUT BUTTER

For the full recipe, reduce the cream cheese to ½ package (4 oz/113 g) and reduce the confectioners' sugar to 2 cups (8 oz/227 g). Add 1⅓ cups (12 oz/340 g) smooth peanut butter. For the half recipe, reduce the cream cheese to ¼ package (2 oz/58 g) and reduce the confectioners' sugar to 1 cup (4 oz/113 g). Add ⅔ cup (6 oz/170 g) smooth peanut butter.

### BROWN SUGAR

For the full recipe, use 2 cups (14 oz/397 g) packed dark brown sugar in place of 2 cups (8 oz/227 g) of the confectioners' sugar. For the half recipe, use 1 cup (7 oz/198 g) packed dark brown sugar in place of 1 cup (4 oz/113 g) of the confectioners' sugar.

### HONEY

Eliminate the vanilla extract. For the full recipe, use ½ cup honey (6 oz/170 g) in place of 2 cups (8 oz/227 g) of the confectioners' sugar. For the half recipe, use ¼ cup honey (3 oz/85 g) in place of 1 cup (4 oz/113 g) of the confectioners' sugar.

### CRANBERRY JAM

Make the frosting. Then, for the full recipe, stir 1 cup (10 oz/283 g) jarred cranberry jam into the frosting. For the half recipe, stir in ½ cup (5 oz/142 g) jarred cranberry jam.

*bittersweet chocolate ganache*

### full recipe
*makes 5 cups*
*(50 1/3 oz/1.41 kg)*

20 oz (567 g) **bittersweet chocolate**, chopped

¼ teaspoon **table salt**

3⅓ cups (28⅓ oz/805 g) **heavy cream**

¼ cup (2 oz/57 g) **bourbon** or water

### half recipe
*makes 2 1/2 cups*
*(25 oz/709 g)*

10 oz (283 g) **bittersweet chocolate**, chopped

Pinch of **table salt**

1⅔ cups (14⅛ oz/397 g) **heavy cream**

2 tablespoons **bourbon** or water

**1.** In a large bowl, combine the chocolate and salt. In a medium saucepan set over medium-high heat, bring the cream to a boil, stirring occasionally. (Alternatively, you can do this in the microwave in a heatproof measuring cup or bowl in 30-second increments.) Pour the cream over the chocolate, add the bourbon, or water, and whisk until well blended and smooth. Chill, stirring occasionally, until thick and very cold, about 3 hours, or cover with plastic and refrigerate up to 5 days

**2.** Scrape the chilled chocolate mixture into the bowl of a stand mixer fitted with the whisk attachment. Beat on medium-high speed until firm peaks form, 1 to 2 minutes. Cover with plastic and keep at room temperature until ready to use.

*flavor swaps*

### MILK CHOCOLATE

For the full recipe, use 20 ounces (567 g) good-quality milk chocolate in place of the bittersweet chocolate and 2⅔ cups (22⅝ oz/642 g) heavy cream in place of the 3⅓ cups heavy cream. For the half recipe, use 10 ounces (283 g) good-quality milk chocolate in place of the bittersweet chocolate and 1⅓ cups (11⅜ oz/322 g) heavy cream in place of the 1⅔ cups heavy cream.

### WHITE CHOCOLATE

For the full recipe, use 24 ounces (681 g) good-quality white chocolate in place of the bittersweet chocolate and 2⅔ cups (22⅝ oz/642 g) heavy cream in place of the 3⅓ cups heavy cream. For the half recipe, use 12 ounces (340 g) good-quality white chocolate in place of the bittersweet chocolate and 1⅓ cups (11⅜ oz/322 g) heavy cream in place of the 1⅔ cups heavy cream.

### ESPRESSO

For the full recipe, add 2 tablespoons instant espresso powder to the chocolate before adding the hot cream. For the half recipe, add 1 tablespoon instant espresso powder to the chocolate before adding the hot cream.

*vanilla marshmallow frosting*

### full recipe

*makes 5 cups*
*(22 oz/624 g)*

2 cups (14 oz/397 g) **granulated sugar**

6 large **egg whites**, at room temperature

½ cup (5¼ oz/149 g) **light corn syrup**

½ teaspoon **table salt**

2 teaspoons **pure vanilla extract**

### half recipe

*makes 2¹/₂ cups*
*(11 oz/312 g)*

1 cup (7 oz/198 g) **granulated sugar**

3 large **egg whites**, at room temperature

¼ cup (2⅝ oz/74 g) **light corn syrup**

¼ teaspoon **table salt**

1 teaspoon **pure vanilla extract**

Arrange the bowl of a stand mixer on top of a pot of simmering water set over medium-low heat (the water shouldn't touch the bottom of the bowl). Combine the sugar, egg whites, corn syrup, and salt in the bowl. Whisk lightly and constantly until the sugar is dissolved and reaches 170°F (80°C) on an instant-read thermometer, 7 to 9 minutes. Remove the bowl from the pot and place it on the stand mixer fitted with the whisk attachment. Add the vanilla and beat on medium-high speed until the mixture holds medium-firm peaks (the tip will bend slightly at the top) when the beater is lifted, 7 to 10 minutes. The frosting will still feel warm; use immediately.

## vanilla pastry cream

*makes 2³/₄ cups (28 oz/794 g)*

½ cup (3½ oz/99 g) **granulated sugar**

¼ cup (1¼ oz/35 g) **cornstarch**

¼ teaspoon **table salt**

3 large **egg yolks**

1 large **egg**

2¼ cups (18¼ oz/511 g) **whole milk**

3 tablespoons (1½ oz/ 42 g) **unsalted butter**, cut into small cubes, softened

2 teaspoons **pure vanilla extract**

In a medium saucepan, combine the sugar, cornstarch, and salt. Add the egg yolks and egg and whisk until well blended and lighter in color. Whisk in the milk. Whisking constantly, bring to a boil over medium-low heat, 1 to 3 minutes. Cook, whisking constantly, for 1 minute more. Remove the pan from the heat, whisk in the butter and vanilla, and scrape the mixture into a medium bowl. Press a piece of plastic wrap directly onto the surface of the pastry cream to prevent a skin from forming and refrigerate it until cold, at least 2 hours. Before using, stir until smooth.

### LIGHTENED PASTRY CREAM

Make the Vanilla Pastry Cream, chill it, and stir until smooth. Whip ⅓ cup (2⅞ oz/82 g) heavy cream until stiff peaks form when the beater is lifted, then fold into the pastry cream.

*flavor swaps*

### BOOZY

Use 2 to 3 teaspoons liquor of your choice (dark rum, Kahlúa, Bailey's Irish Cream, etc.) in place of the vanilla extract.

### BUTTERSCOTCH

Use an equal amount of dark brown sugar in place of the granulated sugar. Use 2 to 3 teaspoons scotch whiskey in place of the vanilla extract.

## vanilla mascarpone cream frosting

### full recipe
*makes about 6 cups*
*(26³/₈ oz/748 g)*

2 cups (17 oz/482 g) **heavy cream**, chilled

⅔ cup (5⅓ oz/148 g) **mascarpone**

1 cup (4 oz/114 g) **confectioners' sugar**, sifted

1 tablespoon **pure vanilla extract**

Pinch of **table salt**

### half recipe
*makes about 3 cups*
*(13¹/₈ oz/372 g)*

1 cup (8½ oz/241 g) **heavy cream**, chilled

⅓ cup (2⅝ oz/74 g) **mascarpone**

½ cup (2 oz/57 g) **confectioners' sugar**, sifted

1½ teaspoons **pure vanilla extract**

Pinch of **table salt**

In the bowl of a stand mixer fitted with the whisk attachment, combine the cream, mascarpone, confectioners' sugar, vanilla, and salt and beat on medium-low speed until blended and smooth, about 1 minute. Increase the speed to medium high and beat until firm peaks hold when the beater is lifted, 1 to 2 minutes. Use immediately or store well covered for up to 3 days in the refrigerator. Before using, gently fold the chilled cream to combine.

## flavor swaps

### NUTELLA

#### full recipe
Increase the amount of cream to 2⅔ cups (22⅝ oz/642 g). After beating, fold in 1 cup (10 oz/283 g) hazelnut spread, such as Nutella.

#### half recipe
Increase the amount of cream to 1⅓ cups (11⅜ oz/322 g). After beating, fold in ½ cup (5 oz/142 g) hazelnut spread, such as Nutella.

### MOCHA

#### full recipe
Increase the amount of cream to 2½ cups (21¼ oz/603 g). Add ½ cup (1½ oz/42 g) unsweetened natural cocoa powder and 1 teaspoon instant espresso powder (optional).

*continued*

## MOCHA (CONT.)

### half recipe

Increase the amount of cream to 1¼ cups (10⅝ oz/301 g). Add ¼ cup (¾ oz/20 g) unsweetened natural cocoa powder and ½ teaspoon instant espresso powder (optional).

## FRUIT PUREE

### full recipe

After beating the cream, fold in 2 cups (16 oz/454 g) well-chilled fruit puree.

### half recipe

After beating the cream, fold in 1 cup (8 oz/228 g) well-chilled fruit puree.

## JAMMIN'

### full recipe

After beating the cream, fold in 1 cup (11 oz/312 g) fruit jam or marmalade.

### half recipe

After beating the cream, fold in ½ cup (5½ oz/156 g) fruit jam or marmalade.

## MAPLE

### full recipe

Reduce the amount of cream to 1⅓ cups (11⅜ oz/322 g). Use 1 cup (11 oz/312 g) pure maple syrup in place of the confectioners' sugar.

### half recipe

Reduce the amount of cream to ⅔ cup (5⅝ oz/159 g). Use ½ cup (5½ oz/156 g) pure maple syrup in place of the confectioners' sugar.

## TIRAMISÙ

### full recipe only

Add 5 tablespoons coffee liqueur and 1 tablespoon instant espresso powder along with the other ingredients.

## BOOZY

### full recipe only

Add 5 tablespoons liqueur of your choice (Amaretto, Grand Marnier, etc.) along with the other ingredients.

## whipped caramel cream

### full recipe

*makes about 5 cups*
*(40³/₄ oz/1155 g)*

2 cups (20 oz/567 g)
**Caramel Sauce**
(page 160), well chilled

1½ cups (12¾ oz/361 g)
**heavy cream**, chilled

1 cup (8 oz/227 g)
**mascarpone**

Pinch of **table salt**, plus
more as needed

### half recipe

*makes about 2¹/₂ cups*
*(20³/₈ oz/577 g)*

1 cup (10 oz/283 g)
**Caramel Sauce**
(page 160), well chilled

¾ cup (6⅜ oz/181 g)
**heavy cream**, chilled

½ cup (4 oz/113 g)
**mascarpone**

Pinch of **table salt**, plus
more as needed

In the bowl of a stand mixer fitted with the whisk attachment, combine the sauce, cream, mascarpone, and a pinch of salt and beat on medium-low speed until blended and smooth, about 1 minute. Increase to medium-high speed and beat until firm peaks hold when the beater is lifted, 1 to 2 minutes. Taste and add more salt as desired. Use immediately or store well covered in the refrigerator for up to three days. Before using, gently fold the cream to combine.

*whipped lemon curd cream*

### full recipe

*makes about 6 cups
(38 oz/1078 g)*

1½ cups (12⅛ oz/360 g)
**heavy cream**, chilled

1 cup (8 oz/227 g)
creamy **goat cheese**,
preferably with citrus
notes, or **mascarpone**

Pinch of **table salt**

2 cups (18 oz/511 g)
**Lemon Curd** (page 159),
well chilled

### half recipe

*makes about 3 cups
(19 oz/539 g)*

¾ cup (6 oz/180 g)
**heavy cream**, chilled

½ cup (4 oz/113 g)
creamy **goat cheese**,
preferably with citrus
notes, or **mascarpone**

Pinch of **table salt**

1 cup (9 oz/255 g)
**Lemon Curd** (page 159),
well chilled

In the bowl of a stand mixer fitted with the whisk attachment, combine the cream, goat cheese, and salt and beat on medium-low speed until blended and smooth, about 1 minute. Increase to medium-high speed and beat until firm peaks hold when the beater is lifted, 1 to 2 minutes. Add the lemon curd and, using a spatula, fold in until just blended. Use immediately or store well covered for up to three days in the refrigerator. Before using, gently fold the chilled cream until blended.

## white chocolate frosting

### full recipe

*makes about 5 cups
(32 oz/908 g)*

4 sticks (2 cups/
16 oz/454 g) **unsalted
butter**, at room
temperature

2 cups (8 oz/227 g)
**confectioners' sugar**,
sifted

1 tablespoon **pure
vanilla extract**

¼ teaspoon **table salt**

8 oz (227 g) good-
quality **white chocolate**,
melted and slightly
cooled

### half recipe

*makes about 2¹/₂ cups
(16 oz/454 g)*

2 sticks (1 cup/8 oz/
227 g) **unsalted butter**,
at room temperature

1 cup (4 oz/113 g)
**confectioners' sugar**,
sifted

1½ teaspoons **pure
vanilla extract**

⅛ teaspoon **table salt**

4 oz (113 g) good-quality
**white chocolate**, melted
and slightly cooled

In the bowl of a stand
mixer fitted with the
paddle attachment,
beat the butter on
medium speed until
smooth, about 1 minute.
Add the confectioners'
sugar, vanilla, and
salt and beat on
medium-high speed
until well blended,
about 2 minutes. Add
the white chocolate
and beat until well
blended and fluffy,
about 1 minute more.
Cover with plastic
wrap and store at room
temperature until
ready to use or for
up to 2 days. Before
using, bring to room
temperature and whisk
until smooth and warm
enough to spread.

## flavor swaps

### COCONUT

For the full recipe,
reduce the vanilla to
2 teaspoons and add
½ teaspoon coconut
extract. For the half
recipe, reduce the
vanilla to 1 teaspoon and
add ¼ teaspoon coconut
extract.

### PEPPERMINT

For the full recipe,
reduce the vanilla
to 2 teaspoons and
add ½ teaspoon pure
peppermint extract or
oil. For the half recipe,
reduce the vanilla
to 1 teaspoon and
add ¼ teaspoon pure
peppermint extract
or oil.

AMERICAN BUTTERCREAM FROSTINGS

*vanilla buttercream frosting*

### full recipe

*makes about 5 cups
(44$\frac{1}{8}$ oz/1.25 kg)*

¼ cup (1⅛ oz/32 g)
**unbleached all-purpose
flour**

1⅓ cups (10⅘ oz/320 g)
**whole milk**

1½ cups (10½ oz/298 g)
**granulated sugar**

½ teaspoon **table salt**, plus
more to taste

5 sticks (2½ cups/
1¼ pounds/567 g)
**unsalted butter**, at room
temperature

2 to 3 tablespoons **pure
vanilla extract**

### half recipe

*makes about 2$\frac{1}{2}$ cups
(22 oz/624 g)*

2 tablespoons **unbleached
all-purpose flour**

⅔ cup (5⅖ oz/160 g)
**whole milk**

¾ cup (5¼ oz/149 g)
**granulated sugar**

¼ teaspoon **table salt**, plus
more as needed

2½ sticks (1 cup plus
4 tablespoons/10 oz/
283 g) **unsalted butter**,
at room temperature

1 to 2 tablespoons **pure
vanilla extract**

**1.** Place the flour in a small saucepan. Tipping the
pan to one side, add about 2 tablespoons of the
milk and whisk until the mixture forms a thick,
smooth paste. Add another 2 tablespoons milk and
whisk until blended. Set the pan on the counter and
gradually add the remaining milk, whisking until the
mixture is smooth.

**2.** Place the pan over medium heat and, whisking
constantly, bring the mixture to a boil. Cook,
continuing to whisk constantly, for 1 minute.
Remove the pan from the heat, add the sugar and
measured salt, and whisk until the sugar is dissolved.

**3.** Pour the mixture through a fine-mesh sieve set
over a medium bowl (do not press down). Scrape
the underside of the sieve into the bowl and
discard the floury remnants in the sieve. Set aside,
stirring occasionally, to cool completely. (For faster
cooling, set the bowl over a larger bowl filled with
ice and a little water, stirring and scraping the sides
frequently until chilled to room temperature.)

**4.** In the bowl of a stand mixer fitted with the
paddle attachment, beat the butter on medium
speed until smooth, about 1 minute. Add the cooled
sugar mixture and 2 tablespoons of the vanilla
and beat on medium speed until smooth and well
blended, about 2 minutes more. If the mixture looks
grainy or "broken," keep mixing until the texture
is smooth. Taste and add more salt and vanilla as
needed. The flavor should be vibrant.

**5.** Store the buttercream, well covered or in
heavy-duty zip-top bags with the air pushed out, in
the refrigerator for up to 4 days or in the freezer
for up to 3 months. Before using, bring to room
temperature and beat until smooth and light.
Before using, bring to room temperature and whisk
until smooth and warm enough to spread.

## DOUBLE CHOCOLATE

### full recipe

Use 2 tablespoons all-purpose flour and ⅔ cup (2 oz/57 g) unsweetened natural cocoa powder in place of the all-purpose flour. Cook as directed. Combine 1⅓ cups (8 oz/227 g) chopped bittersweet chocolate and the vanilla in a heatproof medium bowl. Pour the sugar mixture through a fine-mesh sieve set over the chocolate and stir until the chocolate is melted. (If necessary, microwave or set the bowl over gently simmering water.)

### half recipe

Use 1 tablespoon all-purpose flour and ⅓ cup (1 oz/28 g) unsweetened natural cocoa powder in place of the all-purpose flour. Cook as directed. Combine ⅔ cup (4 oz/113 g) chopped bittersweet chocolate and the vanilla in a heatproof medium bowl. Pour the sugar mixture through a fine-mesh sieve set over the chocolate and stir until the chocolate is melted. (If necessary, microwave or set the bowl over gently simmering water.)

## BOOZY

### full recipe

Use 4 to 5 tablespoons of the liquor of your choice (Bailey's Irish Cream, dark rum, hazelnut liqueur, bourbon, Grand Marnier, etc.) in place of the vanilla extract.

### half recipe

Use 2 to 2½ tablespoons of the liquor of your choice in place of the vanilla extract.

## ESPRESSO

### full recipe

Add 5 teaspoons instant espresso powder to the flour along with the other ingredients. Use an equal amount of light brown sugar in place of the granulated sugar.

### half recipe

Add 2½ teaspoons instant espresso powder to the flour along with the other ingredients. Use an equal amount of light brown sugar in place of the granulated sugar.

## COCONUT

### full recipe

Use an equal amount of coconut milk in place of the whole milk. Add 1 tablespoon pure vanilla extract and 2 teaspoons coconut extract. Stir ⅔ cup (1⅝ oz/46 g) sweetened shredded coconut into the frosting.

### half recipe

Use an equal amount of coconut milk in place of the whole milk. Add 1½ teaspoons pure vanilla extract and 1 teaspoon coconut extract. Stir ⅓ cup (⅞ oz/25 g) sweetened shredded coconut into the frosting.

## MALTED MILK

### full recipe

After beating, stir 1 cup (4½ oz/128 g) malted milk powder into the buttercream.

### half recipe

After beating, stir ½ cup (2¼ oz/64 g) malted milk powder into the buttercream.

*frostings and fillings*

*continued*

## NUT

### full recipe

Combine 1 cup (4 oz/ 113 g) finely chopped toasted nuts in the saucepan along with the flour. Use an equal amount of firmly packed light brown sugar in place of the granulated sugar. For a smooth buttercream, strain the mixture and discard the nuts or, for a chunky texture, leave the nuts in the buttercream. Proceed as directed using only 1 tablespoon vanilla.

### half recipe

Combine ½ cup (2 oz/ 57 g) finely chopped toasted nuts in the saucepan along with the flour. Use an equal amount of firmly packed light brown sugar in place of the granulated sugar. For a smooth buttercream, strain the mixture and discard the nuts or, for a chunky texture, leave the nuts in the buttercream. Proceed as directed using only 1½ teaspoons vanilla.

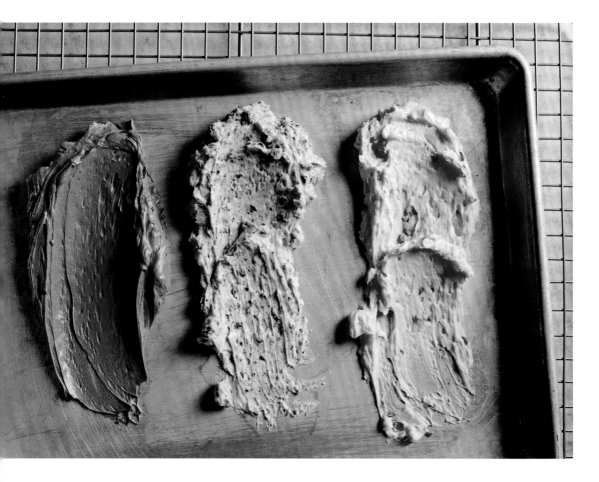

Any of the following can be stirred into batches of any of the frostings.

## COOKIE CRUMBS

*full recipe*

Stir ½ cup (2 oz/57 g) ground cookies (any flavor) into the frosting.

*half recipe*

Stir ¼ cup (1 oz/28 g) ground cookies (any flavor) into the frosting.

## CRUSHED FRUIT

*full recipe*

Fold 2 cups (10 oz/ 283 g) lightly crushed fresh fruit into the frosting.

*half recipe*

Fold 1 cup (5 oz/142 g) lightly crushed fresh fruit into the frosting.

## CHOCOLATE CHIPS

*full recipe*

Stir 1 cup (6 oz/170 g) finely chopped chocolate or mini chips (bittersweet, milk, or white) into the frosting.

*half recipe*

Stir ½ cup (3 oz/85 g) finely chopped chocolate morsels or mini chips (bittersweet, milk, or white) into the frosting.

## NUTS

*full recipe*

Stir 1 cup (4 oz/120 g) finely chopped toasted nuts (of your choice) into the frosting.

*half recipe*

Stir ½ cup (2 oz/60 g) finely chopped toasted nuts (of your choice) into the frosting.

## CITRUS

*full recipe*

Stir 3 tablespoons finely grated orange or lemon zest into the frosting.

*half recipe*

Stir 1½ tablespoons finely grated orange or lemon zest into the frosting.

## GINGER

*full recipe*

Stir ½ cup (2¼ oz/64 g) finely chopped crystallized ginger into the frosting.

*half recipe*

Stir ¼ cup (1⅛ oz/32 g) finely chopped crystallized ginger into the frosting.

# soaks, glazes, sauces, and accompaniments

CLASSIC SOAK

¼ cup (1¾ oz/50 g)
**granulated sugar**

⅓ cup (2⅞ oz/74 g) **water**

In a small saucepan over medium-low heat, or in a heatproof container in the microwave for 15-second increments, combine the sugar and water and cook until the sugar is dissolved. Set aside to cool to room temperature. (For faster cooling, set the bowl over a larger bowl filled with ice and a little water, stirring frequently.) Store the soak, covered, for up to 2 days in the refrigerator or for up to 3 months in the freezer.

*flavor swaps*

**CREAM**   Use ⅓ cup (2⅞ oz/82 g) heavy cream in place of the water and stir in ½ teaspoon pure vanilla extract after cooking.

**CHOCOLATE**   Add 1 tablespoon unsweetened natural cocoa powder after cooking and stir until dissolved.

**COFFEE**   Add 2 tablespoons coffee liqueur and ¾ teaspoon instant espresso powder after cooking and stir until dissolved.

**BOOZY**   Add 2 tablespoons liquor of your choice after cooking.

**CITRUS**   Use ¼ cup (2 oz/57 g) fresh lemon or orange juice in place of the water and stir in 1 tablespoon lemon or orange extract (optional) after cooking.

**PEPPERMINT**   Add ¼ teaspoon pure peppermint extract or oil after cooking.

*makes about*
**¹/₂ cup**
*(4¹/₂ oz/128 g)*

3 oz (85 g) **bittersweet** or **milk chocolate**, chopped (½ cup)

¼ cup (2⅛ oz/60 g) **heavy cream**

1 tablespoon **golden cane syrup** or **light corn syrup**

Combine the chocolate, cream, and cane syrup in a small heatproof bowl and melt over a pan of simmering water, or in a heatproof container in the microwave for 15-second increments, stirring until smooth, about 4 minutes. Remove from the heat and set aside until cooled and thickened, about 1 hour. Store covered in the refrigerator for up to 2 weeks and reheat before using. It can also be heated and served warm or at room temperature as a sauce.

### *flavor swaps*

**MILK CHOCOLATE** ◦ Use an equal amount of milk chocolate in place of the bittersweet chocolate and proceed as directed.

**WHITE CHOCOLATE** ◦ Use 5 ounces (142 g) chopped white chocolate in place of the bittersweet chocolate and proceed as directed.

BITTERSWEET CHOCOLATE GLAZE OR SAUCE

*makes ²/₃ cup*
(5⁷/₈ oz/167 g)

1 stick (½ cup/4 oz/113 g) **unsalted butter**, cut into pieces

¾ cup (5¼ oz/149 g) **granulated sugar**

⅔ cup (5⅜ oz/152 g) fresh **lemon juice**

1 tablespoon finely grated **lemon zest**

¼ teaspoon **table salt**

3 large **eggs**

3 large **egg yolks**

**1.** In a large saucepan, melt the butter over medium heat for 1 to 2 minutes. Remove the pan from the heat and whisk in the sugar, lemon juice, zest, and salt. Whisk in the eggs and yolks until well blended. Return the pan to medium-low heat and cook, whisking constantly, until the mixture coats a spatula and holds a line drawn through it with a finger and is 175°F (80°C), 5 to 7 minutes. Don't let the mixture boil or the eggs will curdle.

**2.** Using a fine-mesh sieve, strain the curd over a medium bowl, without pressing on the zest (and any bits of curdled egg). Scrape the outside of the strainer into the bowl and discard the solid remains. Cover the surface of the curd with plastic wrap and refrigerate until chilled, about 3 hours or up to 2 weeks. (For faster cooling, scrape into a bowl set over a larger bowl filled with ice and a little water, stirring and scraping the sides frequently.)

LEMON CURD

*makes about*
**2 cups**
(18 *oz*/511 *g*)

1⅓ cups (11⅜ oz/322 g) **heavy cream**

1½ cups (10½ oz/298 g) **granulated sugar**

½ cup (4¼ oz/113 g) **water**

½ teaspoon **table salt**, plus more as needed

**1.** In a small saucepan over medium heat, or in a heatproof container in the microwave for 30-second increments, heat the cream until very warm.

**2.** Combine the sugar and water in a medium saucepan. Cook over low heat, stirring, until the sugar is dissolved and the mixture is boiling, about 4 minutes, then stop stirring and increase the heat to high. When the sugar begins to caramelize, swirl the pan until the caramel turns deep amber, 2 to 3 minutes. Continue to gently swirl the pan over the heat to even out the caramel color. Remove the pan from the heat and carefully add the warmed cream; it will sputter. Whisk until the caramel is completely smooth. Add the measured salt, and whisk until blended. Taste and add more salt as desired. Let the caramel cool, stirring frequently, until room temperature. Refrigerate until chilled, about 60 minutes. Store covered in the refrigerator for up to 2 weeks. Serve at room temperature or slightly warm.

*makes* **2 cups**
(22 oz/642 g)

# MAPLE GLAZE

1 cup (4 oz/113 g) **confectioners' sugar**, sifted

¼ cup (2¾ oz/79 g) **pure maple syrup**, plus more as needed

¼ teaspoon **pure maple extract** (optional)

Stir together the confectioners' sugar, the measured maple syrup, and the maple extract in a small bowl. Add more syrup, a little at a time, until the glaze is smooth, very thick, and shiny; it should fall from the spoon into a thick ribbon. Just before serving, drizzle the glaze over the cake.

*makes* ¹/₂ *cup*
(6³/₄ *oz/191 g*)

1 (1-inch [2 centimeter]-thick) block of **bittersweet, semisweet, milk**, or **white chocolate**

**1.** Line a half-sheet pan with parchment. Firmly slide the blade of a vegetable peeler down the narrow side edge of the chocolate block, letting the chocolate curls fall onto the parchment. If you're getting only small broken pieces, the chocolate is too cold. Microwave it (on a paper towel) on medium power in 5-second increments. If the chocolate gets too warm, pop it (on a paper towel) into the refrigerator to chill for a few minutes before continuing.

**2.** Once you have enough curls, slide the pan into the refrigerator for a few minutes to firm up any softened chocolate. Fold the parchment around the chocolate shavings to fashion a chute and pour the shavings into a container or zip-top bag. Cover and store in the refrigerator for up to 6 months.

CHOCOLATE CURLS

## DOUBLE BERRY SAUCE

**BLUEBERRIES, RASPBERRIES, BLACKBERRIES** (halved, if large), and strawberries (cut into ½- to ¾-inch pieces) can be used to make this sauce. Adjust the sugar, zest, and juice as needed.

4 cups (20 oz/567 g) fresh **berries**, rinsed and dried

⅔ cup (4⅝ oz/131 g) **granulated sugar**, plus more as needed

2 teaspoons fresh **lemon, lime**, or **orange juice**, plus more as needed

1 teaspoon finely grated **lemon, lime**, or **orange zest**, plus more as needed

Pinch of **table salt**

Combine 1½ cups (7½ oz/213 g) of the berries, the measured sugar, lemon juice, lemon zest, and salt in a medium saucepan. Cook over medium heat, stirring frequently, until the sugar is dissolved and boiling, about 1 minute. Reduce the heat to low and simmer, stirring frequently, until the berries are soft and the liquid is syrupy, 2 to 3 minutes. Remove the pan from the heat and add the remaining 2½ cups (12½ oz/354 g) berries. Set aside to cool, stirring occasionally, to room temperature. Cover and refrigerate until chilled, about 2 hours or up to 1 week. For faster cooling, set the bowl over a larger bowl filled with ice and a little water, stirring and scraping the sides frequently.

*makes* **2¹/₂ cups** (25 *oz*/709 *g*)

# acknowledgments

As my fellow authors would likely attest, writing a cookbook is a journey, and this one was no exception. It truly takes a team of rock stars to make a book come alive, and I am deeply grateful for the combined efforts of all the folks on Team Sheet Cake.

A special thanks goes out to the always effervescent Chris Hoelck and Juli Roberts. They masterfully produced, developed, and tested many of these cakes, and their insights and suggestions proved invaluable. It's a blessing to count them as friends as well as trusted colleagues.

I first worked with my agent, Rica Allannic, on a revision of *The Joy of Cooking*. Riding that roller coaster proved we could survive any publishing situation. Thanks, Rica, for sharing your in-depth knowledge of cookbook publishing. Your guidance, wisdom, and support got me through this ride. On to the next!

What readers don't see when turning the pages of a cookbook is the countless hours of dedicated hard work that goes on behind the scenes to produce a project like this one. I'm grateful for all the talented art, design, editorial, marketing, and production teams at Clarkson Potter for creating this lovely book.

Thank you to Francis Lam and Aaron Wehner for leading an all-star team and for supporting this project. I am honored to add this book to your list.

Special thanks to my editor, Michele Eniclerico, for gracefully and effortlessly taking on this project and steering it home. Your enthusiasm, patience, and positivity meant the world to me.

Sending major kudos to production editor Patricia Shaw for guiding this book through the uncharted waters of a global pandemic. I can only imagine it took superhuman effort.

Stephanie Huntwork created the beautiful design of this book. Thank you—inside and out, it's gorgeous and exactly as I imagined it.

Many thanks to food photographer Lauren Volo and food stylist Monica Pierini for using their magical talents to create the glorious, happy images that bring these recipes to life.

Beyond grateful for Erica Gelbard, PR guru and my sister-in-cake. Looking forward to baking side-by-side one of these days!

Sending loving appreciation to my fellow bakers. We've met and baked together for years, in real life as well as virtually, and I have cherished and grown from our shared experiences both as a baker and as a human. No matter how near or far we live from one another, you guys dole out buckets of laughter, friendship, and support.

Lastly and lovingly, my deepest thanks to Chris, Alex, and Tierney.

# index

Note: Page references in *italics* indicate photographs.

# Conversion Chart

*Equivalent Imperial and Metric Measurements*

American cooks use standard containers, the 8-ounce cup and a tablespoon that takes exactly 16 level fillings to fill that cup level. Measuring by cup makes it very difficult to give weight equivalents, as a cup of densely packed butter will weigh considerably more than a cup of flour. The easiest way therefore to deal with cup measurements in recipes is to take the amount by volume rather than by weight. Thus the equation reads:

1 cup = 240 ml = 8 fl. oz.  1/2 cup = 120 ml = 4 fl. oz.

It is possible to buy a set of American cup measures in major stores around the world.

In the United States, butter is often measured in sticks. One stick is the equivalent of 8 tablespoons. One tablespoon of butter is therefore the equivalent to ½ ounce/15 grams.

## LIQUID MEASURES

| FLUID OUNCES | U.S. | IMPERIAL | MILLILITERS |
|---|---|---|---|
|  | 1 teaspoon | 1 teaspoon | 5 |
| ¼ | 2 teaspoons | 1 dessertspoon | 10 |
| ½ | 1 tablespoon | 1 tablespoon | 14 |
| 1 | 2 tablespoons | 2 tablespoons | 28 |
| 2 | ¼ cup | 4 tablespoons | 56 |
| 4 | ½ cup |  | 120 |
| 5 |  | ¼ pint or 1 gill | 140 |
| 6 | ¾ cup |  | 170 |
| 8 | 1 cup |  | 240 |
| 9 |  |  | 250, ¼ liter |
| 10 | 1¼ cups | ½ pint | 280 |
| 12 | 1½ cups |  | 340 |
| 15 |  | ¾ pint | 420 |
| 16 | 2 cups |  | 450 |
| 18 | 2¼ cups |  | 500, ½ liter |
| 20 | 2½ cups | 1 pint | 560 |
| 24 | 3 cups |  | 675 |
| 25 |  | 1¼ pints | 700 |
| 27 | 3½ cups |  | 750 |
| 30 | 3¾ cups | 1½ pints | 840 |
| 32 | 4 cups or 1 quart |  | 900 |
| 35 |  | 1¾ pints | 980 |
| 36 | 4½ cups |  | 1000, 1 liter |
| 40 | 5 cups | 2 pints or 1 quart | 1120 |

## SOLID MEASURES

| U.S. AND IMPERIAL MEASURES | | METRIC MEASURES | |
|---|---|---|---|
| OUNCES | POUNDS | GRAMS | KILOS |
| 1 |  | 28 |  |
| 2 |  | 56 |  |
| 3½ |  | 100 |  |
| 4 | ¼ | 112 |  |
| 5 |  | 140 |  |
| 6 |  | 168 |  |
| 8 | ½ | 225 |  |
| 9 |  | 250 | ¼ |
| 12 | ¾ | 340 |  |
| 16 | 1 | 450 |  |
| 18 |  | 500 | ½ |
| 20 | 1¼ | 560 |  |
| 24 | 1½ | 675 |  |
| 27 |  | 750 | ¾ |
| 28 | 1¾ | 780 |  |
| 32 | 2 | 900 |  |
| 36 | 2¼ | 1000 | 1 |
| 40 | 2½ | 1100 |  |
| 48 | 3 | 1350 |  |
| 54 |  | 1500 | 1½ |

## OVEN TEMPERATURE EQUIVALENTS

| FAHRENHEIT | CELSIUS | GAS MARK | DESCRIPTION |
|---|---|---|---|
| 225 | 110 | ¼ | Cool |
| 250 | 130 | ½ |  |
| 275 | 140 | 1 | Very Slow |
| 300 | 150 | 2 |  |
| 325 | 170 | 3 | Slow |
| 350 | 180 | 4 | Moderate |
| 375 | 190 | 5 |  |
| 400 | 200 | 6 | Moderately Hot |
| 425 | 220 | 7 | Fairly Hot |
| 450 | 230 | 8 | Hot |
| 475 | 240 | 9 | Very Hot |
| 500 | 250 | 10 | Extremely Hot |

Any broiling recipes can be used with the grill of the oven, but beware of high-temperature grills.

## EQUIVALENTS FOR INGREDIENTS

all-purpose flour—plain flour
baking sheet—oven tray
buttermilk—ordinary milk
cheesecloth—muslin
coarse salt—kitchen salt
cornstarch—cornflour
eggplant—aubergine

granulated sugar—caster sugar
half and half—12% fat milk
heavy cream—double cream
light cream—single cream
lima beans—broad beans
parchment paper—greaseproof paper
plastic wrap—cling film

scallion—spring onion
shortening—white fat
unbleached flour—strong, white flour
vanilla bean—vanilla pod
zest—rind
zucchini—courgettes or marrow